Crossing Borders, Crossing Boundaries

Crossing Borders, Crossing Boundaries

The Role of Scientists in the U.S. Acid Rain Debate

Leslie R. Alm

PRAEGER

Westport, Connecticut
London

Library of Congress Cataloging-in-Publication Data

Alm, Leslie R., 1950–
    Crossing borders, crossing boundaries : the role of scientists in the U.S. acid rain debate
/ Leslie R. Alm.
        p.   cm.
    Includes bibliographical references and index.
    ISBN 0–275–96916–9 (alk. paper)
        1. Acid rain—Environmental aspects—United States.   2. Acid rain—Environmental
aspects—Canada.   3. Environmental policy—United States.   4. Environmental
policy—Canada.   5. Scientists—United States—Political activity.   6.
Scientists—Canada—Political activity.   I. Title.
    TD195.5.A45   2000
    363.738′6—dc21   99–088624

British Library Cataloguing in Publication Data is available.

Library of Congress Catalog Card Number: 99–088624
ISBN: 0–275–96916–9

First published in 2000

Praeger Publishers, 88 Post Road West, Westport, CT 06881
An imprint of Greenwood Publishing Group, Inc.
www.praeger.com

Printed in the United States of America

The paper used in this book complies with the
Permanent Paper Standard issued by the National
Information Standards Organization (Z39.48–1984).

10 9 8 7 6 5 4 3 2

For Melvin

Contents

Preface

John Kingdon, noted scholar and author of one of the most cited works on American public policy (*Agendas, Alternatives, and Public Policies*), has argued that because policy makers must make decisions in a world of uncertainty, they turn to scientists for guidance and answers. However, Kingdon has also suggested that there are limits to the solutions that science can provide, because there are those who distrust the work of scientists and because, in the end, it is the policy makers who must make the final decisions as to what is the best solution. Some scholars and practitioners agree with Kingdon and contend that the value judgments needed to make policy decisions belong only in the realm of politics and not in the realm of science. Others maintain that this simply is an impossibility.

I have been studying the relationship between science and policy making in the environmental context for some time. The development of a transboundary air pollution policy (centered on the problem of acid rain) between the United States and Canada provides an excellent case study of how science (and scientists) affect the making of environmental policy. Acid rain concerns did not emerge as a policy issue until scientific research into the basic nature of the problem became available. Scientists were responsible for defining the acid rain issue and setting the context in which the debate took place. Yet, during the policy debate on acid rain, the scientific community did not speak with one voice. There were bitter policy debates within the scientific community, and the science of acid rain proved to be a very contentious subject as Canada attempted to persuade the United States to act.

While many scholars have emphasized the primacy of politics in the acid rain debate and critiqued the science-policy linkage, little has been written from the scientists' point of view. My work does exactly that: It provides a chance for the scientists themselves to express their feelings about their role in the policy-making process. Furthermore, because the United States acid rain issue is inherently linked to the Canadian acid rain problem, my study articulates the views of both United States and Canadian scientists as gleaned from surveys and interviews conducted over three different time periods between 1989 and 1997.

There exists a need to know more about how scientists view the policy-making process, because they play such an important role in introducing, popularizing, and elevating ideas that directly affect environmental policy debates. Understanding the role of science (and scientists) is critical to understanding why environmental policies either succeed or fail. Scientists' perceptions are especially meaningful in the case of the United States–Canada acid rain debate because, from the very beginning of this policy debate, scientists were called upon to communicate the scientific facts and uncertainties objectively and to describe the expected outcomes. Essentially, the scientific community was expected to provide the best available science to determine the causes and effects of acid rain and how to control it. Because serious questions remain about the role that scientists played in the development of our present day acid rain policies and because scientists will continue to play a central role in the implementation of such policies in the United States and Canada, it is worth our while to explore how scientists view the making of these policies.

Furthermore, understanding the relationship between scientists and policy making, especially in the area of environmental policy studies, is one of the hottest new directions in policy research. Recently, for example, the National Science Foundation created a new National Center of Environmental Decision-Making, whose primary missions are to understand the interface between science and public policy and find better ways to link public policy to the efforts of the environmental science community. In addition, the newly created Commission for Environmental Cooperation (CEC), under the auspices of the North American Agreement on Environmental Cooperation (NAAEC), is attempting to further the establishment of cooperative technical and policy linkages for North American environmental management among environmental scientists, environmental advocacy organizations, and governments.

In completing this research, I have benefited from the advice and counsel of many scholars. In this regard, Charles Davis, Steven Mumme, Don Alper, Everett Cataldo, Alan Schwartz, and Marc Simon have provided essential insights into the environmental policy-making process. I would especially like to thank Don Munton, not only for his guidance but for the amount and quality of his work in the area of United States–Canadian environmental policy making. He provided me with a foundation and direction as I approached my work.

I thank Dan Abele, the Canadian Embassy, the Idaho State Board of Education, James Weatherby, Stephanie Witt, and Boise State University for their financial support of my research agenda. I would also like to thank Ross Burkhart, Scott Warren, Leah Taylor, and Greg Raymond for their assistance.

Above all, I wish to thank my wife Barbara for being the one true guiding light in all that I do.

Chapter 1

The Science-Policy Linkage and Acid Rain

INTRODUCTION

Acid rain occurs when sulfur and nitrogen oxides emitted by such sources as coal-fired power plants and automobiles are transported hundreds of miles in the atmosphere and returned to earth as acid compounds.[1] Acid rain has been linked to serious environmental damage and was the subject of a decade-long policy debate within the United States as well as the major focal point of an often bitter and contentious policy debate between the United States and Canada. The policy debate in the United States ended with the passage of the Clean Air Act Amendments in November of 1990. The policy debate between the United States and Canada ended with the signing of *The Agreement Between the Government of Canada and the Government of the United States of America on Air Quality* (commonly referred to as the Air Quality Accord) in March of 1991.

Several fine books have already been written about the policy debate that encompassed the establishment of both a United States domestic policy and a bilateral agreement between the United States and Canada on acid rain.[2] Although these books present an intriguing and illustrative look at the development of a North American acid rain policy, none of them focuses exclusively on the science-policy linkage that so permeated the debate over acid rain at both the domestic and bilateral levels. That is the purpose of this book.

The depiction of the acid rain policy debate that follows builds on the foundation set forth by the many studies of the environmental policy-making process that have been completed over the past decade. (Among others, see Bocking 1997; Harrison and Hoberg 1994; Lee 1993; Rosenbaum 1998; Sarewitz 1996; and Williams and Matheny 1995.) These studies have highlighted the complex and controversial aspects of linking science to policy. Generally speaking, the science-policy nexus has been characterized by scholars as a treacherous place to be, because environmental issues have compelled public officials to make scientific judgments and scientists to resolve policy issues, and neither group is trained to make such judgments (Rosenbaum 1998, 126). Furthermore, this tension between scientists and policy makers appears to be emblematic of all environmental policy making. As Walter Rosenbaum has observed: "The almost inevitable need to resolve scientific questions through the political process and the problems that arise in making scientific and political judgments compatible are two of the most troublesome characteristics of environmental politics" (1998, 126).

The release of the final assessment report of the National Acid Precipitation Assessment Program (NAPAP) in November of 1991 is illustrative of Rosenbaum's concerns. NAPAP was initiated under the Acid Precipitation Act of 1980 to provide a compilation of the best available scientific, technological, and economic information relevant to making policy decisions about acid rain (U.S. National Acid Precipitation Assessment Program 1991, i). At the time of its inception, there were high hopes that this congressionally mandated 10-year program would provide policy makers with scientific consensus regarding the causes and effects of acid rain as well as lay the basis for informed political decisions and public acceptance of the final acid rain policy outcome (Russell 1992, 107).

It would be nice to report that soon after acid rain was identified as a transboundary air pollution problem worthy of attention, the scientific community, under the direction of NAPAP, took the lead and produced a consensus opinion regarding a possible solution. That did not happen. NAPAP, which spent over $600 million and employed thousands of research scientists, published its final report in November of 1991, almost one year *after* the 1990 Clean Air Act Amendments (with Title IV dealing specifically with acid rain) were signed into law.[3]

Following this sequence of events, many scientists were highly critical of United States acid rain policy making, especially as it pertained to NAPAP. There were charges of political interference with the course of science and delays in the release of first-class science that did not support political agendas (Schindler 1992, 124). Individual scientists were accused of acting out of self-interest, using hyperbole and selective data to support policy positions, and —outright—advocating policy without clearly distinguishing between policy and science (Perhac 1991a, 38).

Questions were raised about the policy relevance of NAPAP's scientific findings. Scientists asked why, if the science was so important, had it had such a modest influence on the legislative process (Loucks 1993, 72; Perhac 1991a, 38; Roberts 1991, 1302)? Even more immoderate—to American scientists— were charges that the acid rain debate (especially as it pertained to NAPAP) had led to the loss of a substantial measure of scientific credibility. There were even accusations that the policy debate over acid rain had resulted in United States science being perceived as a "laughingstock" by the international scientific community (Schindler 1992, 125).

On a more positive note, some scientists argued that most of the key scientific findings of NAPAP had been available to decision makers well before final action was taken (Russell 1992, 109). Others argued that the scientific findings and policy assessments provided by NAPAP were very important and had provided substantial guidance for making decisions about transboundary air pollution (Cowling 1992, 111). Nevertheless, for the most part, the science of acid rain and the scientists who participated in the acid rain debate were cast in an unfavorable light. What follows is the story of how this unfavorable opinion came about.

THE PURPOSE OF THIS BOOK

The purpose of this book is fairly straightforward. It is to provide a description and analysis of the science-policy linkage that defined the policy debate over acid rain in the United States. In the study of the interaction between scientists and policy makers, the science-policy linkage encompasses the timing and nature of those interactions, the influence of each set of actors on the others, and the effect of the interaction on the policy process and eventual policy outputs of government. In essence, the study of the science-policy linkage is concerned with answering such questions as when, where, and why scientists enter the policy-making process and what effect they have.

Along these lines, a secondary goal of this book is to highlight an often ignored view of the policy process, that of natural scientists. Previous research of the policy process has been written and viewed almost exclusively from the point of view and interpretation of social scientists. This study was completed with the full intent of allowing natural scientists a chance to express their views of the way the environmental policy-making process works. This was done by focusing on large, philosophical questions that have been the subject of many scholarly inquiries: questions about whether it is possible for scientists to be truly objective in completing their research and whether scientists can be advocates for environmental action while remaining within the bounds of the scientific process.

It was also the intent of this study to explore differences between how natural scientists and social scientists view the tensions between science and policy. As delineated below, much has been made of the difference between the ways in which social scientists and natural scientists approach their work and I wanted to see how this played out with respect to their views on the science-policy linkage.

Furthermore, I wanted to distinguish differences and highlight similarities between United States and Canadian scientists, since much of the acid rain debate was carried out in the context of transborder pollution, with the Canadians taking an active role in United States policy making. Canadian scientists testified at congressional hearings in the United States and corresponded directly with United States policy makers. Moreover, as established by the Air Quality Accord, there has been a substantial increase in the number of contacts and cooperative projects involving scientists from both countries.

Finally, in exploring the science-policy linkage in the context of the acid rain debate, I wanted to discuss the large, philosophical questions concerning advocacy, objectivity, and the separation of science and policy. I believe that these questions are pertinent not only to the making of environmental policy today, but that they will remain pertinent in the long term. Two events have recently put the science-policy linkage at the forefront of concern. First, the North American Free Trade Agreement has created new transboundary institutions (e.g., the Commission for Environmental Cooperation) that are looking for policy guidance on how to deal with a wide range of transboundary environmental problems in North America.[4] In this regard, the Commission for Environmental Cooperation is attempting to further the establishment of cooperative technical and policy linkages for North American environmental management among environmental scientists, environmental advocacy organizations, and governments. Second, the National Science Foundation has created a new National Center for Environmental Decision-Making whose primary missions are to understand the interface between science and public policy and to find better ways to link public policy to the efforts of the environmental science community.

The following chapters will provide a description of the acid rain debate as it played out over the decade of the 1980s. To understand the role that scientists played in the development of the United States acid rain policy, it is important to understand the full evolution of that policy. Furthermore, if science is to be truly linked to environmental policy making in a meaningful manner, it is essential to look back and see why it took so long for policy makers to reach the same conclusion that some of our best scientists had reached very early in the policy debate. Moreover, understanding the part that science played in reaching the policy agreement over acid rain may provide guidance in dealing with future environmental concerns.

SCIENTISTS IN THE POLICY MAKING PROCESS

The questions raised by the critics of science's role in the policy debate over acid rain go right to the heart of the dilemma posed by Rosenbaum in the opening paragraphs of this book. How do policy makers resolve scientific questions through the political process while making scientific and political judgments compatible? It is not an easy question to answer. Furthermore, attempting to answer this question leads directly to a series of additional questions. When, where, and how should scientists enter the policy-making process? Do policy makers listen to the advice of scientists? Is it really possible for scientists to provide objective analyses of their research results? Is it possible for scientific research to be separated from policy judgments?

Many scholars, in attempting to answer these questions (for a broad array of policy issues), have commented on the role of science and scientists in the policy process. The work of scientists has been characterized as the most powerful of all forms of knowledge (Gregory and Miller 1998, 248) and as the only publicly acceptable rationale for policy making (Wildavsky 1995, 5). In this regard, some scholars caution that the importance of science and scientists in relation to the making of public policy should never be underestimated. Kai N. Lee has pointed out that "Without the centralizing vision of science . . . we cannot perceive the planet we share with other living things. . . . When science yields unambiguous negative implications for significant public values, action should be taken by governments. . . . When science yields consensus on the importance of a problem, however ambiguous the existing knowledge may be, governments should consider action" (1993, 183–84).

Science and scientists have been cited as especially important to environmental policy making. Both Rosenbaum (1998, 152) and Mark Rushefsky (1995, 283) observed that because scientific issues so permeate environmental problems, the substantial involvement of scientists in making environmental policy is essential. Karen Litfin described scientists as important political actors, because they are the first to discover environmental problems and, hence, are instrumental in defining how the problems are conceptualized and which policy options should be addressed (1994, 9). Steven Yearley noted that some environmental issues (like reduction in stratospheric ozone) would not even exist without scientific input (1995, 462).

Yet, with all the importance allocated to science and scientists, questions remain about the ability of scientists to connect to a policy world that eventually relies on politicians to make the final policy decisions, with or without scientific input (Kingdon 1995, 57). Scientists and policy makers are said to work in two different worlds, each deeply rooted in divergent human occupations. As Lee pointed out, "Science and politics serve different purposes. Politics aims at the responsible use of power; in a democracy, 'responsible' means accountable, eventually to voters. Science aims at finding truths—results that withstand the scrutiny of one's fellow scientists" (1993, 163).

Within the context of environmental policy making, scientists and policy makers are supposed to be isolated from each others' influence, with barriers maintained such that scientists can complete their research with careful adherence to the canons of the scientific process, and policy makers can be protected from scientists telling them what they should decide (Russell 1992, 108). In essence,

[t]he responsibility of scientists . . . in a democracy is to understand and clearly communicate the scientific facts and uncertainties and to describe expected outcomes objectively. Deciding what to do involves questions of societal values where scientists, as scientists . . . have no special authority. . . . The proper role for scientists . . . is to provide advice and counsel . . . to those who are charged by our society to make policy decisions. It is not a proper role for a scientist . . . as such, to seek to make (or even to have special influence on) societal decisions. (Cowling 1992, 113–14)

What these scholars are speaking about is a boundary between scientists and policy makers that functions as a description of concrete agreements and as a metaphor for relationships. In this context, boundaries are viewed as more than just a construct depicting borders between countries or borders between disciplines.   Boundaries are viewed as being about relationships and the constructs that define those relationships.[5] As important as the crossing of international borders is to the acid rain issue,[6] it is the crossing of the boundary that exists between scientists and policy makers that provides students of environmental policy making with an exciting point of contemplation.

METHODS AND DATA

As stated above, the purpose of this book is to provide a description and analysis of the science-policy linkage that so permeated the policy debate over acid rain in the United States.   To accomplish this task, I focused on four specific criticisms of science (and scientists) made during the acid rain policy debate: that policy makers did not view the science as relevant; that science and policy were not clearly distinguished from each other; that scientists acted out of self-interest to advocate for specific policy outcomes; and that scientists abandoned one of the main tenets of the scientific process, objectivity, in pushing for specific policy options.

Multiple sources were used to gather information for this study.   Scholarly work involving acid rain was reviewed along with government documents and reports. Among the most valuable sources of information were the transcripts of the hearings held on acid rain in the United States Congress.[7]   In addition, information for this study was obtained from both mail surveys and on-site interviews of United States and Canadian policy elites over four different time periods: spring and summer of 1989, spring and summer of 1992, summer and fall of 1995, and spring, summer and fall of 1997.[8]

In 1989, I gathered data from 51 interviews and 139 survey responses (62 percent response rate) on the perceptions of policy elites.[9] Those interviewed and surveyed were actors directly involved in the acid rain debate in both Canada and the United States, with a focus on four specific groups: government officials (U.S. = 42; Canada = 13), representatives of the coal, utility, and smelting industries (U.S. = 32; Canada = 5), representatives of environmental groups (U.S. = 24; Canada = 6), and researchers and scientists (U.S. = 46; Canada = 12).

In 1992, I gathered data from 51 interviews and 144 survey responses (60 percent response rate) on the perceptions of policy elites.[10] Those interviewed and surveyed were actors directly involved in the acid rain debate in both Canada and the United States, with a focus on four specific groups: government officials (U.S. = 33; Canada = 12), representatives of the coal, utility, and smelting industries (U.S. = 30; Canada = 9), representatives of environmental groups (U.S. = 30; Canada = 8), and researchers and scientists (U.S. = 46; Canada = 24).[11]

In 1995, information was gathered from natural scientists only. I surveyed 100 United States natural scientists (return rate of 60 percent) and 100 Canadian natural scientists (return rate of 69 percent) regarding the formulation of acid rain policy in North America. All the natural scientists who participated in this survey were directly involved in acid rain research for each of their respective countries.

The 1997 Interviews

The heart of the data for this study, however, comes from the interviews I conducted from March through November of 1997. Over this time period, I asked 129 scientists to respond to four questions about the science-policy linkage as it pertained to the criticisms delineated above.[12]

- Do policy makers listen to scientists?
- Should scientists advocate policy positions?
- Is it possible to separate science from policy making?
- Is it possible for scientists to be objective in completing their research?

Of the 129 scientists interviewed, 66 were natural scientists (33 each from the United States and Canada) and 63 were social scientists (32 from the United States and 31 from Canada).[13]

The Natural-Social Science Dichotomy

The term "natural-social science dichotomy" is used for two basic reasons. First, as Jean-Guy Vaillancourt has pointed out, "Environmental problems are considered to be the social aspects of natural problems, and the natural aspects of social problems" (1995, 218). Second, previous research has suggested that differences exist between how natural scientists and social scientists perceive the science-policy linkage.[14] A number of scholars have carefully documented evidence that scientists' disciplinary backgrounds influence their approaches to research questions and to evidence, leading to divergent interpretations of specific data and different ways of combining information. (See Ashford 1995, 612; Bimber 1996, 7–12; Bocking 1997, 5–6; Graham, Green, and Roberts 1988, 187; Harrison and Hoberg 1994, 33; and Lynn 1986, 48.) Others have argued that a gap often divides the social sciences and humanities from the physical and biological sciences such that social scientists are not accorded the same status as natural scientists. (See Hagan 1994, 853; Pielke 1997, 262; Sarewitz 1996, 26; James Smith 1991, 14; and P. Stern, Young, and Druckman 1992, 25.) In addition, Helen Ingram, H. Brinton Milward, and Wendy Laird have pointed out that in dealing with environmental policy, natural scientists often portray themselves as outside the political process and as poorly understood by politicians, while social scientists find that natural scientists wield a great deal more influence than they admit (1990, 5).

Natural scientists' perceptions are important because, from the very beginning of the policy debate over acid rain, they were called upon to communicate scientific facts and uncertainties and describe the expected outcomes following the best scientific methodologies. Their perceptions are also important because serious questions remain about the part they played in the development of acid rain policy and because they will continue to play a central role in the implementation of the tenets set forth by the 1990 Clean Air Act Amendments and the Air Quality Accord.

Social scientists' perspectives are important because they offer special insight into the environmental policy-making process as it has played out in the establishment of an acid rain policy. As documented earlier, the efforts of social scientists have resulted in countless manuscripts, essays, reports, analyses, and books describing the intricacies involved in passing United States legislation and producing the bilateral agreement between the United States and Canada regarding acid rain. Social scientists are in a unique position to observe and comment in a systematic and comprehensive way on the everyday workings of the science-policy linkage. In short, social scientists provide us with important documented information that sheds light on the way the science-policy linkage should (and actually does) work.

The United States–Canada Dichotomy

The term "United States–Canadian dichotomy" is used for two basic reasons. First, much of the policy debate over acid rain in the United States was connected to the bilateral policy debate between Canada and the United States over transborder air pollution. In fact, the formulation of a United States domestic policy on acid rain was completed only after a long and drawn-out policy debate between the United States and Canada that was considered "a giant among all U.S.–Canadian environmental problems" (Curtis and Carroll 1983, 32). Moreover, this cross-border debate was so all-encompassing, it "overshadowed almost all other elements of the bilateral relationship" between the United States and Canada (Schwartz 1994, 489).

Second, and more important, the United States–Canada division permits testing whether different social and political contexts affect the views of scientists in each country in regard to the canons of the scientific process. Previous research findings have suggested that the acid rain policy debate was marked by considerable mistrust between United States and Canadian scientists because of the politicization of the acid rain issue and its different significance in each country (Alm 1997, 352–54). It appears that despite extensive collaboration between United States and Canadian scientists, each country responded differently to its cross-border air pollution problems. In fact, it has been asserted that the political controversy created by these different views was not only a handicap to joint United States–Canadian scientific research, but defined a clear and drastic mismatch between what politics needs and what science can offer (Forster 1993, 4).

It is also important to note that scientists in each country function under two distinct types of policy making. The Canadian approach relies heavily on scientific judgment and limits public debate about the scientific basis of policy decisions, while the United States approach is characterized by open conflict over regulatory science, including public debate over the interpretation of scientific evidence. Furthermore, Canadian officials tend to place a greater emphasis on the truth-seeking character of science, whereas in the United States, the regulatory process places greater emphasis on the value-laden policy components of science (Harrison and Hoberg 1994, 168–84).

If this research finds that the social and political contexts of scientists affect the way they perceive the scientific world, it would support the view that the values and institutions of science are already highly penetrated by national and social values and governmental institutions. If the outcome of this research is that no substantial difference exists between United States and Canadian scientists' views of the science-policy linkage, it would offer further evidence of the separation of the worlds of science and politics. Moreover, it would suggest that the institutions of science may be stronger and more independent of social and national concerns than they are generally given credit for in today's world.

The Scientists Interviewed

The majority of the scientists interviewed worked for universities (U.S. = 66%; Canada = 66%) or the government (U.S. = 31%; Canada = 33%). Three were working for private industry. All of the scientists interviewed had earned their doctorates (Ph.D.) except for one United States natural scientist who had two master's degrees in forest ecology, and two social scientists (one from the United States and one from Canada) who had earned their master's degrees and had extensive work-related experience in environmental policy making.

The natural scientists interviewed all met one or more of the following criteria: testimony given at congressional or parliamentary hearings on acid rain, participation in reviewing the National Acid Precipitation Assessment Program, service on the task force implementing the Canada–United States Air Quality Accord, or published, peer-reviewed scientific research on acid deposition or in an area related to acid deposition. The natural scientists interviewed were represented by a wide range of disciplines, including chemistry (15), atmospheric science (13), biology (16), ecology (8), forestry (3), engineering (6), and geology (5).

Because the number of social scientists working specifically on acid rain policy in both the United States and Canada is quite limited, the social scientists interviewed for this study were chosen because they were directly involved in teaching, researching, or working in environmental policy making. The social scientists interviewed were represented by a wide range of disciplines, including political science (28), economics (9), international studies (4), public administration and policy (10), history (2), sociology (2), and environmental studies (8).

THE ACID RAIN POLICY DEBATE

The Scientists

The story that follows documents the role that scientists played in the acid rain debate during the decade of the 1980s. Early in this policy debate, some of the most respected and prestigious United States scientists produced what they viewed as scientific consensus in many of the areas related to acid rain and argued that adequate scientific information existed to begin controls (Driscoll et al. 1985). Yet, the results of their efforts did not prove compelling enough for policy makers in the United States to take immediate action to reduce acid rain pollution. Frustrated with this lack of action, many of these scientists became policy advocates for the reduction of acid rain pollutants. During the acid rain policy debate, many scientists crossed over the accepted professional boundaries that define their disciplines, despite the possible negative consequences within the scientific community.

As will be illustrated in the coming chapters, debate among scientists first brought the acid rain issue into international prominence, and scientific research catapulted acid rain into a major North American environmental concern. Further, scientists proved essential to keeping the acid rain issue in front of both the public and policy makers. From 1973 to 1978, only 19 scientific reports were completed on acid rain in the United States. But in 1979, the number of scientific reports on acid rain rose to 10 and continued to rise to a peak of 44 reports in 1983.[15] And from 1980 through 1988, over 150 scientists presented testimony about acid rain at congressional hearings.[16] More important, however, scientists were responsible for generating interest in acid rain through their very public statements concerning the scientific understanding of acid rain and the consequences of various policy options.

Simply put, scientists became very active participants in the public debate over acid rain. Whether scientists were reluctantly pulled into the debate or joined it willingly, the outcome was the same: the science of acid rain became so politicized that scientists ended up having to defend both their science and their methods in the public forum.[17] Furthermore, once scientists crossed the established boundary between scientific analysis and policy advocacy, there was no returning. The science (and scientists) became so entangled within the policy debate over acid rain that, by the mid-1980s, one observer argued that beyond the immediate issue of acid rain, something ugly and potentially disastrous had occurred. In the words of Roy Gould, the science of acid rain had been "increasingly misrepresented and distorted for political ends. The scientific community . . . felt the chilling effect of politics to a degree unprecedented in recent times. Acid rain will have had a silver lining if it forces us to confront and reverse this ominous trend toward the politicization of science" (1985, 5).

The Canadians

However, scientists were not the only group to cross an established boundary of behavior during the policy debate over acid rain. Members of the Canadian government also crossed a boundary that had long existed between Canada and the United States with respect to engagement in foreign policy issues. The foreign policy instrument historically used in the United States–Canada relationship has been the traditional diplomatic one, one that offers the advantages of "confidentiality, considerable trust and the mutual commitment to resolving day to day issues that constitute the bread and butter of a bureaucratic relationship" (Clarkson 1983, 12). As Don Munton and Geoffrey Castle made abundantly clear: "Taking up issues of concern to one side or the other through formal diplomatic channels rather than pursuing them through public, less co-operative avenues is one of the unwritten norms of Canadian-American relations" (1992, 322).[18]

Yet, Canadians disregarded this unwritten norm and plunged headlong into the United States domestic policy debate over acid rain. Canadians reacted to stalemate in the official diplomatic negotiations by taking their argument directly to the United States Congress and the United States public. They conducted what some have labeled "diplomacy with an attitude" (Munton 1997b, 16). In the end, Canada had to back off from such a frontal attack on the United States policy-making system and conduct its business out of sight and behind the scenes. It has been suggested that the effectiveness of Canada's efforts was very limited (Munton 1997b, 11). But, it has also been suggested that Canada's efforts helped convince the United States to act on acid rain far sooner than it ever would have on its own (Doran 1997, 171).[19] What is not questioned is that Canada kept the acid rain issue at the top of its bilateral agenda with the United States and that Canada made every effort to make sure the United States was aware of that fact.

Moreover, just as scientists were willing to cast aside the norms expected of those within the scientific community, the Canadians were willing to cast aside the norms expected of their diplomatic relationship with the United States. Furthermore, the possible consequences of casting these norms aside were (and still are) quite severe. Scientists who cross over into the political side of a policy debate risk losing their status in the scientific community. Their credibility and reputation as scientists can be greatly diminished, jeopardizing their ability to make further credible contributions to the policy process. Similarly, countries that move beyond the accepted norms of diplomatic procedures in the United States risk condemnation and may even come under attack for failing to abide within specified domestic laws and policies.[20] Yet, both scientists and Canadians were willing to take these risks in an attempt to convince United States policy makers that they had to act to reduce transboundary acid rain pollution. This is one of the facts that makes this study of the United States acid rain policy debate so interesting.

The United States and Canada: A Special Relationship

The United States and Canada have a long-standing and often-cited record of successfully resolving environmental disputes (Schmandt, Clarkson, and Roderick 1988, 187).[21] Moreover, it has been argued that the relatively large number of common institutional linkages, coupled with the common cultural characteristics of language, open and free exchange of information, and a professional diplomatic ethic, create a mutual responsiveness that serves to resolve the major differences between the two countries (Munton 1980–81, 142–43).[22] Indeed, much has been made of what some call "the closest and most cordial transboundary relationship between any two countries in the world" (Chamberlin and Legault 1997, 3).

But to characterize the Canadian-American interdependence only in these terms is to underestimate the depth and complexity of the relationship between these countries. A certain asymmetry of power, economic development, and population size has always distinguished the United States–Canadian bilateral relationship (Chamberlin and Legault 1997, 5). From the very beginning of the policy debate, a substantial series of imbalances, particularly regarding transboundary air pollution, characterized this relationship (Carroll 1982, 2–3; Munton 1980–81, 166). Whereas 50 percent (or more) of Canada's acid deposition comes from sources in the United States, only about 15 percent of United States deposition comes from Canadian sources. In addition, a much higher percentage of Canadian territory than of United States territory is vulnerable to acid deposition. Further, because Canada has such a high dependence on forest products (and acid rain is viewed as a serious threat to the health of forests), it is economically much more vulnerable than the United States to the effects of acid rain. Finally, American and Canadian publics differ in their level of awareness about transboundary air pollution; Canadians appear to be more knowledgeable about the issue than Americans.

At times, there has also been a tendency on the part of the United States to take Canada for granted (Fry 1988). Early in the debate over transboundary air pollution, warnings against this line of thinking were numerous. Democratic Congressman Michael Barnes of Maryland, a member of the House Committee on Foreign Affairs, cautioned that even though "the United States and Canada have a long history of the most cordial and friendly relations . . . this does not mean we can take our Canadian friends for granted" (U.S. Congress, House of Representatives, Committee on Foreign Affairs, Subcommittee on Human Rights and International Organizations 1981, 1).[23] New York Senator Daniel Moynihan reflected this sentiment: "It is so easy to think of Canada as a neighbor and some how subsumed under the same set of concerns that we have, and what ever we are doing they are doing, tracking each other in one way or another. That is not so, not at all" (U.S. Congress, Senate, Committee on Foreign Relations, Subcommittee on Arms Control, Oceans, International Operations and Environment 1982, 3).

The asymmetry in the United States–Canadian environmental sphere is also documented by previous research investigating attitudes of Canadians and Americans. Scholars have shown that Canadians are not only more sympathetic to environmental protection but more supportive of environmental regulation (Steel et al. 1990, 388–91). Others have suggested that Canadians tend to perceive higher risks from acid rain pollution than do their American counterparts (Steger et al. 1988, 747–64), that Canadians are more likely to believe that both the United States and Canada are responsible for the pollution (Pierce et al. 1989, 21), and that Canadians have a greater appreciation for the degree of scientific and technological collaboration needed to deal with problems such as transboundary air pollution (Winegard 1991, 4–5).

Further, while some scholars have described a new era of cooperation between the United States and Canada represented by "a more integrated effort within both governments to mobilize the bilateral relationship" (Kirton 1993, 286), others have insisted that Canada has become increasingly dependent on the United States with respect to the quality of its environment (Munton and Castle 1992, 313) and that "sharing the border is an uneven experience, one that has fallen mainly to Canadians, who have reason to pay more attention to the relationship. But cordial relations cannot be taken for granted, and future accord will depend on Americans making an effort to understand the Canadian view" (McKinsey and Konrad 1989, 31).[24]

In any case, it must be recognized that Canada is a sovereign nation, quite independent and different from the United States.[25] There are not only great differences between the historical perspectives of Canada and the United States, but significant differences between the countries' political cultures and environmental regulatory regimes as well (Chapin 1988; Harrison and Hoberg 1994, 8–13; Steger et al. 1987, 3).[26] The inclination to treat the bilateral relationship between the United States and Canada in a casual manner is not a wise one. In fact, as John Carroll noted, "it is both inaccurate and perhaps dangerous to go as far as both peoples do in taking the bilateral relationship for granted" (1986, 1).

A FRAMEWORK OF STUDY

This study used the policy process set forth by John Kingdon (1995) to organize, describe, and highlight certain aspects of the acid rain policy debate in the United States. In his work, Kingdon described a process whereby political problems emerge and rise on the governmental agenda for action. He defined a governmental agenda, which includes issues to which government officials are paying attention, and a decision agenda, which includes those issues within the governmental agenda that are being considered for active decisions (1995, 3–4). Why some issues make it onto the agendas and others do not can be explained by the confluence of the process streams of problems, policies, and politics (1995, 165–95).[27] Kingdon argued that there are always many problems on which to act, and that rather than a lack of ideas, many potential solutions (policies) exist to deal with these problems. The key to understanding the policy process is being able to explain how particular problems get joined to particular solutions and how a proper political environment allows action on the problem and leads to a solution.

On occasion, problems become so pressing (for example, the energy crisis) that they move easily to the governmental agenda on their own merit. More often, though, problems do not move alone but emerge within the constraints of the political stream. That is, problems are greatly affected by such things as public opinion, the national mood, legislative turnover, and interest-group pressure. Furthermore, to move up to the decision agenda, problems usually must be linked to a politically acceptable solution.

What Kingdon defines as a "policy window" is time when an opportunity exists to link together problems, solutions, and politics (1995, 165). Two factors tend to fleetingly open these windows. One is a change in the problem stream that calls attention to a particular issue—for example, a focusing event or crisis. This is often the case with environmental issues, with events ranging from Three Mile Island to the Exxon Valdez oil spill bringing action on long-standing problems. The other force that opens policy windows is change in the political stream—new coalitions, a change of president or of congressional leadership, mass mobilization by interest groups, or major swings in public opinion. In addition, a person who is highly involved in the policy process can sometimes, through his or her own efforts, join the streams. Such a person is dubbed a policy entrepreneur (Kingdon 1995, 179–83).

For Kingdon, problems and solutions are floating around in problem and policy streams; actors backing particular solutions search for appropriate problems and/or political conditions to increase the likelihood of adoption of those solutions. Within these streams, constant adjustment and adaptation of problems, solutions, and politics occur as a result of the actions of those involved in the policy process (Kingdon 1995, 86–89).

Kingdon's description of the policy process, as outlined above, is particularly helpful in portraying the policy debate over acid rain in the United States. It captures the essence of how policy makers behave in the political arena and highlights a special role for scientists in the policy process. Scientists are described by Kingdon as belonging among the hidden participants who play a significant part in the public policy-making process by working behind the scenes, generating alternatives, proposals, and solutions that pave the way for successful public policy formulation (1995, 68–70).[28] In this regard, scientists are viewed as key actors in loosely knit communities of specialists where, "Ideas bubble around . . . [and] people try out proposals in a variety of ways: through speeches, bill introductions, congressional hearings, leaks to the press, circulation of papers, conversations, and lunches. They float their ideas, criticize one another's work, hone and revise their ideas, and float new versions" (Kingdon 1995, 200).

While scientists may not be responsible for the prominence of problems on the agenda, they play a key role in framing problems within a unique issue context and in setting alternative solutions to those problems. In brief, Kingdon described a policy process in which scientists, through the gradual accumulation of knowledge or the occurrence of scientific discovery, help create a general climate of ideas that affects policy makers' thinking (1995, 55–56). Kingdon alluded to this particular aspect of the policy process as the "long process of softening up the system" (1995, 201).

Kingdon's framework is also helpful in organizing and describing the unique role that Canada played in the development of a United States acid rain policy. The Canadians fought very hard to keep the acid rain issue on the United States governmental agenda and participated willingly in the long process of "softening up the system," as described. The Canadians attempted to frame the acid rain issue in the context of what they perceived as both the problem and the solution. They attempted to guide and influence United States public opinion and national mood through multiple strategies. They also attempted to directly influence legislators and members of interest groups. The Canadians created their own windows of opportunity and tried to take advantage of policy windows that opened up within the United States domestic policy system.

In summary, the ideas of John Kingdon offer a way to organize the discussion of the Canadian connection to the United States acid rain policy debate and to illustrate the tensions between science and policy. If the central questions about the science-policy linkage have to do with when, where, and why scientists enter the policy process and what effect they have (as suggested earlier), then the Kingdon model provides a theoretical framework to guide the search for answers to those questions. When and how scientists can most usefully intervene is a question that can be answered in several places—at the stages of problem formation, solution formation, linkage of problem and solution, creation of political forces necessary to move the problem up the ladder on the agenda, and when linking problem, solution and politics together.

OUTLINE OF THIS BOOK

The following chapters examine how science manifests itself in public policy in a transboundary, environmental, and political context. The focus is on the policy debate over acid rain in the United States and the part that science and scientists played in that debate. Chapter 2 provides an overview of the acid rain policy debate, from President Jimmy Carter's second environmental message in 1979 to the signing of the Clean Air Act Amendments in November of 1990. Chapter 3 describes the role that Canada played in keeping the United States focused on reducing acid rain pollution. Chapter 4 documents the tension between science and politics as scientists and policy makers in the United States attempted to define acid rain in a way that would warrant some type of action (or inaction).

Chapters 5 and 6 focus exclusively on how scientists view the policy-making process with respect to the importance of scientific input. The scientists interviewed answer questions that evolved from the severe criticism of science that followed establishment of a United States acid rain policy: Do policy makers listen to scientists? Should scientists advocate policy positions? Is it possible to separate science from policy making? Is it possible for scientists to be objective in completing their research? The words and perceptions of these scientists provide the gist for the thoughts expressed in Chapter 7, which analyzes the science-policy linkage as it stands today and examines implications for the future.

NOTES

1. Acid rain (or acid precipitation) is the commonly accepted term for acid deposition, which occurs in both wet form (when emissions of sulfur dioxide [SO_2] and nitrogen oxides [NO_x] are transformed into acids in the atmosphere and then fall to earth

as fog, rain, hail, or snow) and dry form (when these acid aerosols are brought to earth by gravity or other nonprecipitative means). It is important to note, as Don Munton (1997b, 2) has made clear, that the term "acid rain" should not be interpreted as the only form of transboundary air pollution. Such pollutants as pesticides, herbicides, and heavy metals are also transported over long distances. In short, it needs to be recognized that the problem of acid rain is part of a general phenomenon of the movement of pollutants through air over long distances and should be viewed as such.

2. See Bryner (1995), Carroll (1982), Cohen (1995), Forster (1993), Gould (1985), Kahan (1986), Regens and Rycroft (1988), Schmandt, Clarkson, and Roderick (1988), and Yanarella and Ihara (1985).

3. This report, titled the 1990 Integrated Assessment Report, provided a summary of the causes and effects of acidic deposition and a comparison of the costs and effectiveness of alternative emission control scenarios.

4. The Commission for Environmental Cooperation is an international organization whose members are Canada, Mexico and the United States. It was created under the North American Agreement on Environmental Cooperation (NAAEC) to address regional environmental concerns, help prevent potential trade and environmental conflicts, and promote the effective enforcement of environmental law.

5. For a thorough discussion of boundaries used in this context, see New (1998).

6. Borders in this sense refer to the fact (as pointed out by Lauren McKinsey and Victor Konrad) that nations continue to be defined by spatial mass, and borders tend to reify the differences between peoples (1989, 2). Borders give a land-based frame of reference to social, cultural, and linguistic differences.

7. From 1979 through 1990, there were 125 congressional hearings held concerning acid rain and 84 acid rain bills introduced (31 in the Senate and 53 in the House). In the House of Representatives, the bulk of the hearings on acid rain were held before the Committee on Energy and Commerce and its Subcommittee on Health and the Environment. In the Senate, most of the hearings were held before the Committee on Environment and Public Works and its Subcommittee on Environmental Protection.

8. Earlier works published by the author and based on these surveys and interviews can be found in the *Journal of Environmental Systems* (1988–89, 1994–95, 1997–98), *American Review of Canadian Studies* (1990), *Journal of Borderlands Studies* (1990, 1993), *Environmental Management* (1993), *The Environmental Professional* (1994), *Government and Policy* (1995), *Science, Technology, & Human Values* (1997), and *Canadian-American Public Policy* (1999).

9. Ten of the survey respondents were also interviewed.

10. Three of the survey respondents were also interviewed.

11. For two of these time periods (1989 and 1992) respondents included United States government officials from environmental committee staffs, members of the International Joint Commission, and administrators from such organizations as the Environmental Protection Agency, the National Acid Precipitation Assessment Program, the Department of Energy, the Office of Technology Assessment, and the Council of Environmental Quality. Canadian government respondents included environmental committee staff members, members of the International Joint Commission, and administrators from such agencies as Environment Canada, the Canadian Consulate General, the Ministry of Natural Resources, and the Department of External Affairs. United States industry respondents included representatives from such organizations as the Edison Electric Institute, the Tennessee Valley Authority, the American Public Power Association, the National Coal Association, and the United Mine Workers. Canadian industry respondents included representatives from such organizations as Inco Limited, Falconbridge Limited, the Ontario Mining Association, and Hydro-Quebec.

Environmental respondents included a wide mix of organizations that lobbied at the national level, organized at the grassroots level, and provided a good deal of information to policy makers, the public, and the media. United States members from such organizations as the Defenders of Wildlife, Natural Resources Defense Council, Sport Fishing Institute, Sierra Club, and Izaak Walton League participated, as did Canadian members from such organizations as the Canadian Coalition on Acid Rain, Canadian Nature Foundation, and Canadian Wildlife Federation. The United States and Canadian researchers and scientists who participated came from government agencies, national laboratories, and universities.

12. I asked these questions understanding that they were large and philosophical in nature. Though the questions were asked in a "yes/no" format, interviewees were asked to explain their views in detail based on their personal experience.

13. There is no claim here that this is a purely random sample from a comprehensive population. However, I believe that it is a sample that is representative of natural scientists working on research related to acid rain and of social scientists whose expertise lies in the environmental arena. Over the past decade, I have been gathering names (from my reading and research) of both natural and social scientists who were involved in environmental issues, especially those pertaining to acid deposition, clean air policy, and United States–Canadian environmental policy making. I used this list to contact possible interviewees via mailings, the Internet, and by phone. Of those I contacted, 58 percent of United States respondents and 61 percent of Canadian respondents agreed to be interviewed. I then proceeded to conduct interviews by phone (40 percent) and in person (60 percent). I spent most of March through November 1997 "on the road" conducting these interviews and made a definite attempt to ensure equal numbers of respondents from the United States and Canada and from both the natural and social science areas. Furthermore, a very wide array of disciplines is represented, as are both university and government scientists, and all geographical areas of the United States and Canada. Finally, all the interviews were conducted solely by the author and the interviewees were guaranteed confidentiality.

14. Following the lead of Daniel Sarewitz, this book defines science as reflecting a social consensus that treats the validity of the scientific method as proven (1996, 4–5). That is, the term "science" refers to the body of existing knowledge and not to the technical activity of scientific research. In this regard, science encompasses all the natural sciences (e.g., physics, chemistry, biology, astronomy, and earth science) and excludes the social sciences (e.g., political science, economics, sociology, and history).

15. This is the author's computation based on data from *The Environment Index*.

16. This is the author's computation based on data from the *CIS Index and Abstracts*.

17. As Ernest Yanarella and Randal Ihara have so aptly put it, "members of the scientific community [saw] their studies become political tokens in the debate while they themselves [became] sometimes willing, sometimes reluctant, political actors in the controversy" (1985, 1).

18. Charles Doran argued that "the commitment to what amounts to intervention into the domestic affairs of friendly neighbors is sometimes undertaken with the best of political intentions and the most elevated of motivations. But, in realistic terms, such wholesale intervention . . . into the affairs of neighbors is a transgression of one of the fundamental rules of diplomacy" (1997, 177).

19. Charles Doran also stated that the Mulroney government's efforts to get the Reagan government to do something about acid rain were "masterful" and that the hyping of acid rain as a single issue (in the U.S. view) "turned out to be greatly successful for Canada, obtaining for its expenditure of a magnitude not otherwise to be expected on a

matter upon which the United States was vulnerable but also potentially quite recalcitrant" (1997, 167–68).

20. Kim Richard Nossal contended that "preaching to the Americans" always runs the risk of causing a deterioration of relations and that Americans in particular want to decide for themselves "what is good and right and just" (1997, 192).

21. In this regard, William Winegard stated that "Few Canadians and fewer Americans understand or appreciate the degree of collaboration and cooperation that has grown between both countries in our mutual pursuit of science and technology" (1991, 4).

22. While Don Munton (1997a, 1997b) and others (including the author) continue to view Canada–United States relations in a bilateral context, some scholars believe that because so many interests intersect in the integrated North American economic space and so many people are important participants in the interaction of the two societies, the relationship between the United States and Canada may now be too complex to be characterized as merely bilateral (Leyton-Brown and Sands 1997, 165).

23. Cyrus Vance, Secretary of State in the Carter administration, echoed these sentiments as follows: "Despite the importance of our relations with Canada, however, Americans have often taken Canada for granted. . . . Whatever the cause, the tendency to take Canada for granted is a grave mistake" (1983, ix).

24. Other scholars have made this same argument. John Herd Thompson and Stephen Randall spoke of the asymmetry in the United States–Canada bilateral relationship as reflected by neglect on the American side (1994, 2), and Kenneth Curtis and John Carroll stated, "We believe that good U.S.–Canadian relations depend ultimately on American knowledge and understanding of Canada . . . the greatest knowledge gap exists in the United States; and the magnitude of the U.S.–Canadian relationship must be better understood there in order to receive the commitment it so badly needs" (1983, 93).

25. As W.H. New remarked in his recent analysis of the United States–Canada borderlands: "The obvious fact that societies have separate histories frequently needs restating in order that the fact, and the consequences, of difference do not get ignored" (1998, 41).

26. For a comparative perspective of Canada and the United States in this regard, see Carroll (1991) and L. Jones, Duncan, and Mumme (1997).

27. Kingdon's theory builds on the "garbage can" model of Cohen, March, and Olsen (1972).

28. Among others, Kingdon's hidden cluster of participants includes academics, researchers, career bureaucrats, congressional staffers, and administrative appointees below the top level (1995, 68–70).

Chapter 2

The Politics of Acid Rain: An Overview

INTRODUCTION

In chapter 1, John Kingdon's theoretical framework was established as a point of reference for portraying the development of acid rain as an environmental policy issue in the United States. This chapter uses the ideas set forth by Kingdon to provide an overview of the acid rain issue, from acid rain's initial definition as a problem worthy of governmental attention to the confluence of the problem, political, and policy streams that led to the establishment of a formal policy solution. Along these lines, this chapter uses many of the ideas and institutions that characterize the present-day American political system (e.g., frequent elections, regionalism, presidential-congressional tensions, blockers in Congress) to illustrate why policy makers were led to perceive the cost of action to reduce acid rain pollution as inhibitive.

This chapter outlines the role different United States presidents played in the formulation and passage of the acid rain policy. It is important to recognize how the acid rain issue fared in particular presidential administrations, moving from policy stalemate to policy formulation. In this regard, several windows of opportunity are described, the final passage of acid rain legislation being characterized by changes of leadership in both the executive and legislative branches of government.

Next, it is important to examine the other factors that affected the acid rain policy issue, including economic constraints, regional conflict, and scientific uncertainty. This chapter provides the first glimpse of the role that scientists played in the acid rain policy process as they briefed politicians, testified at congressional hearings, conducted research, and attempted to define acid rain as a serious and legitimate environmental concern.

PRESIDENTAL/CONGRESSIONAL IMPACT

The Beginning of the Debate: The Carter Years

Official recognition of acid rain as a legitimate policy issue within the United States came when President Jimmy Carter, in his second environmental message to Congress in August 1979, identified acid rain as one of the two most serious environmental problems facing the United States (Wetstone 1980, 9).   [The buildup of carbon dioxide in the atmosphere was the other problem named by President Carter.]   As illustrated below, two factors are given most of the credit for bringing about this recognition; the proliferation of scientific studies in the 1970s portraying acid rain as having a detrimental effect on the environment and Canadian pressure for United States action to curb cross-border pollution.

It was scientists who first identified and documented acid rain as a threat to both plant and aquatic life in North America (Cowling 1982, 110–11A) and it was scientists who first brought the acid rain issue to the attention of politicians (Munton 1997a, 328).   Scientists warned of a massive change in environmental conditions whereby acid rain would bring destruction to human and ecological well-being.   They identified sulfur and nitrogen oxides as the dangerous precursors of acid precipitation (Likens et al. 1979, 43) and offered concrete alternatives to limit the emissions of these chemical substances in order to reduce the negative effects of acid rain (Likens 1976, 43–44).   Moreover, scientists also contributed to the increasing anxieties forming over the threat of acid rain by referring to it as "an unpremeditated form of chemical warfare" (Likens, Bormann, and N. Johnson 1972, 40) and "the killing rains" (LaBastille 1979, 9).   As Don Munton has emphasized, "it was the interest and concern of scientists more than broad public knowledge or concern that led to acid rain emerging as a political issue" (1981, 24).

To be sure, scientists did provide American policy makers with hints that acid rain could become a full-blown environmental problem. However, it took overtures from Canada (in combination with scientific evidence) to force the United States to officially recognize acid rain as a policy issue. As early as 1977, Canadian federal environment minister Romeo LeBlanc was calling for the United States to address cross-border pollution (Munton 1997a, 328) and, in 1978, a small group of border-state members of Congress prompted the State Department to open negotiations with the Canadian government concerning acid rain (J. Johnson 1985, 268).   These actions resulted in the formation of a committee (the Bilateral Research Consultation Group) that eventually concluded that acid rain was a serious problem producing irreversible damage to sensitive aquatic ecosystems, and that the United States was responsible for the vast majority of the pollutants that moved across the boundary (Munton 1997a, 329; Munton 1997b, 5–6).   Thus began the Canadian effort to pressure the United States to act and the Carter Administration's commitment to address the issue of acid rain.

In this regard, Environmental Protection Agency (EPA) Administrator Douglas Costle pushed for emission controls. First, he declared that the time had come to make the transition from research to action (Koch 1980c, 1491). Second, using Section 115 of the 1977 Clean Air Act Amendments for guidance, he announced that the United States federal government was authorized to establish emission limitations (Schamndt, Clarkson, and Roderick 1988, 227–29). Costle came to this conclusion after the Canadian Parliament had amended its Clean Air Act in December of 1980 to provide for reciprocity with the United States and had given Ottawa the power to regulate in cases of transboundary pollution. With President Carter calling for action and EPA Administrator Costle leading the charge, it appeared that it would only be a short time before the United States acted to curb its cross-border acid rain pollution. When the Congress of the United States met for its 96th session, all the ingredients seemed to be in place for the establishment of an acid rain policy.

It did not happen. President Carter wavered because of his commitment to increasing the use of coal in meeting the challenge of a perceived energy crisis (D. Davis 1982, 280–87). Costle's call for action immediately became entangled in the courts. District Court Judge Norma Holloway ruled that because the EPA administrator had concluded that acid deposition was endangering public health and the welfare of a foreign country (Canada), federal law required the United States to act. However, this decision was overturned in the federal appeals court in Washington, D.C. (Taylor 1986, 11).[1] The decision to act (or not act) was then left to the United States Congress.

For its part, the members of the 96th Congress reacted to the growing concern over the possible effects of acid rain cautiously by considering actions to reduce acid-forming emissions. Citing the lack of information on the processes by which emissions entering the atmosphere are transformed into harmful acidic compounds, Congress decided to wait for more information from the scientific community before taking action to reduce the precursors of acid rain. What Congress did pass was the Acid Precipitation Act of 1980. This act mandated "a 10-year scientific, technological, and economic study to examine the relationships among fossil fuel combustion, acids and other pollutants formed by emissions, and the effects of these pollutants on the environment, the economy, and human health" (U.S. National Acid Precipitation Assessment Program 1991, 1). With President Carter's reluctance to push for acid rain controls, EPA's request for action tied up in the federal courts, and Congress's initial call for more research before acting, the issue of acid rain was simply passed on to the next administration.

Policy Stalemate: The Reagan Years

The change from the Carter to Reagan administrations had an immediate and lasting impact on the possibility of developing a policy to reduce the emissions that cause acid rain. Reagan came into office determined to shift the responsibility for environmental protection to state and local governments.[2] Responding to what he perceived to be a shift in public priorities, Reagan attempted to reverse course on the federal government's commitment to strong environmental regulation (Mitchell 1984, 51). Accordingly, the Reagan administration proposed legislation to weaken the Clean Air Act. Reagan not only failed to get his legislation passed but was forced to withdraw it under fire. As noted by Evan Ringquist, President Reagan began his first term with the goal of retrenching environmental legislation. After that goal proved impractical because of public opinion and lobbying efforts, he shifted to an administrative strategy of budget and personnel cuts coupled with antienvironmental political appointments and agency reorganizations (1993, 33).

Public opinion polls during Reagan's early years showed that most of the public in both the United States and Canada was concerned about the seriousness of the acid rain problem.[3]   Phillip Roeder and Timothy Johnson noted that surveys taken in the United States and Canada in the period from 1980 to 1984 indicate that between 70 and 90 percent of the public thought that acid rain was a serious problem, or at least as serious as other environmental problems (1985, 64–66).   Both publics ranked acid rain as the fourth most serious of six or more environmental problems.   Other public opinion polls showed that Reagan had gravely mistaken the public's willingness to back off the stringent environmental course set in the 1970s (Mitchell 1984, 54). Moreover, Reagan's antienvironmental policies roused both environmental groups and the Congress to action (Kenski and Kenski 1984, 97–118).

Buoyed by both public opinion results showing the strength of public support for clean air and a massive public relations effort by the Canadians, supporters of acid rain control demanded immediate action. In 1983, led by proposals from Henry Waxman (Democrat, California), Gerry Sikorski (Democrat, Minnesota.), Robert Stafford (Democrat, Vermont), and George Mitchell (Democrat, Maine), over a dozen bills were introduced into Congress to enact controls.   But the ability of opposition forces to delay the proceedings and the effectiveness of Reagan in enacting deep budget cuts in his first term of office thwarted this opportunity to pass legislation (Kenski and Kenski 1984, 115; Mosher 1982, 237–40).

It should be noted that those opposed to acid rain controls had two powerful allies in the United States Congress: Senator Robert Byrd (Democrat, West Virginia) and Congressman John Dingell (Democrat, Michigan).   Byrd, the majority leader of the Senate during most of the 1980s, opposed acid rain legislation that would hurt his West Virginia mining constituents.   Dingell, chairman of the powerful House Committee on Energy and Commerce, wished to limit restrictions placed on the auto industry in terms of fuel efficiency and pollution controls (R. Cohen 1995, 33).

There was also strong opposition to acid rain controls from the coal and utility industries. Carl Bagge, president of the National Coal Association, went so far as to call acid rain "a façade for the forces who would deliberately destroy the carefully-crafted balance of environmental and economic goals that have been achieved by the Clean Air Act during the last decade" (Gould 1985, 36). Dr. Robert Brocksen, representing the Electric Power Research Institute, supported the position that no immediate implementation of sulfur dioxide and nitrogen oxide emission control measures should be instituted because of the complexity and uncertainty of the present scientific research results (Schmandt, Clarkson, and Roderick 1988, 120–22). William Karis, vice president for corporate planning of the Consolidated Coal Company, presented a list of recent scientific papers to Congress showing that "the charge of widespread acid deposition in the United States cannot be substantiated by the evidence" (Kahan 1986, 114).

Based on the stagnation of the acid rain issue in Congress and Reagan's policy of nonaction, it appeared that the lobbying efforts of the coal and utility industries had (at least for the time being) paid off. The momentum to bring about acid rain controls created by the backlash against Reagan's initial attempts to weaken clean air legislation could not be sustained. The Reagan administration then settled into a pattern of obstruction based on the idea that more scientific information was necessary before acid rain controls could be justified (J. Johnson 1985, 271). Although Reagan continued to resist any kind of acid rain legislation during his terms of office, on occasion, events appeared to offer hope for renewed action to reduce acid rain pollution. One such event was the appointment of William Ruckelshaus to the position of EPA administrator in 1983.

The reaction in Congress to this appointment was genuinely optimistic. Spirits soared when Ruckelshaus personally assured all those present at his Senate confirmation hearing that acid rain would be one of his highest priorities and that he would pursue a solution very aggressively (U.S. Congress. Senate. Committee on Environment and Public Works 1983a, 209). Of more significance were the words of President Reagan at Ruckelshaus's swearing-in ceremony on May 18, 1983: "I would like you to work with others in our administration, with the Congress, and with state and local officials to meet this issue [acid rain] head-on" (J. Davis 1983b, 2186). It appeared as if the president had opened the door to acid rain legislation and even made it a top priority of his new EPA administrator. At the time, some observers doubted the sincerity of Reagan's words. Kenski and Kenski warned that the effectiveness of Ruckelshaus would depend on how much support he had from Reagan and that Reagan's past actions did not bode well for Ruckelshaus (1984, 114–15). As it turned out, the doubters were right.

Soon after his appointment, Ruckelshaus appointed a study group that drafted a proposal to reduce emissions by 50 percent. Under immense pressure from the Office of Management and Budget (OMB), Ruckelshaus toned down the report. Even so, he made a modified proposal of reduction to President Reagan. But OMB Director David Stockman and Secretary of Energy Donald Hodel opposed the reduction and successfully blocked Ruckelshaus's plan (J. Davis 1985, 1817; Stanfield 1984, 860). From that point on, Ruckelshaus's testimony in Congress reflected the Reagan position of supporting more study exclusively. For instance, in March 1984, Ruckelshaus testified at both House and Senate hearings that more research was needed to determine if a real problem existed, that he did not find any basis for immediate alarm, and that— on the basis of current scientific knowledge—no additional controls were warranted (U.S. Congress. House of Representatives. Committee on Science and Technology 1984, 16).

Congressional reaction to the Ruckelshaus turnaround was swift and critical. Senator Stafford declared that the hope and encouragement Ruckelshaus portrayed at his swearing-in ceremony were "without genuine foundation" (U.S. Congress. Senate. Committee on Environment and Public Works 1984, 1). Senator Mitchell questioned the personal assurances of integrity, independence, and access to the president, that Ruckelshaus had espoused in his confirmation hearing. Congressman James Scheur was adamant in criticizing Reagan's words of encouragement at Ruckelshaus's swearing-in ceremony as a "sham" and his comments as "all blue smoke and mirrors" (U.S. Congress. House of Representatives. Committee on Energy and Commerce, Subcommittee on Health and the Environment 1983, 27). If the Ruckelshaus appointment had indeed offered a window of opportunity for action on acid rain legislation, that window closed very quickly.

Another event that created an opportunity for movement toward the reduction of acid rain pollution during the Reagan administration was the release of the *Joint Report of the Special Envoys on Acid Rain* in January, 1986. In March of 1985, Prime Minister Brian Mulroney of Canada and President Reagan each agreed to appoint a personal Special Envoy to jointly examine the acid rain issue and prepare a report on their findings, before the prime minister and president met again (scheduled for the spring of 1986). The Special Envoys (Drew Lewis of the United States and William Davis of Canada) published their report in January of 1986. In this report, the Joint Envoys referred to the two most important things they learned:

• Acid rain is a serious environmental problem in both the United States and Canada. Acidic emissions transported through the atmosphere undoubtedly are contributing to the acidification of sensitive areas in both countries. The potential for long-term socioeconomic costs is high.

• Acid rain is a serious transboundary problem. Air pollutants emitted by sources in both countries cross their mutual border, thus causing a diplomatic as well as an environmental problem. (Lewis and W. Davis 1986, 6)

These findings were important on several counts. First, President Reagan's endorsement of this report was his first public acknowledgment that acid rain was a serious environmental problem. Second, Reagan's acceptance of the report committed the United States to a $5 billion control technology demonstration program. Third, the release of the report's findings and Reagan's endorsement of these findings provided a choice opportunity for the members of Congress who supported acid rain controls to promote their agenda.

Joseph Davis reported that with Reagan's public announcement in support of the *Joint Report of the Special Envoys on Acid Rain,* new acid rain bills began appearing on Capital Hill, reflecting renewed interest in the acid rain issue (1986, 675). When Representative Henry Waxman of California submitted his bill on acid rain for consideration, he stated that he wanted to act in the wake of the presidential recognition of the seriousness of the acid rain problem, as represented by Reagan's endorsement of the *Joint Envoys Report* (U.S. Congress. House of Representatives. Committee on Energy and Commerce, Subcommittee on Health and the Environment 1986, 136). Yet, despite Reagan's public pronouncements, there remained a continued threat of a presidential veto on any acid rain legislation. As the congressional session wound to completion in 1986, no acid rain legislation had been brought before the house for a vote. In fact, no acid rain bill would become law during Reagan's time as president.

A Law Is Passed: The Bush Years

Just as the change from the Carter to Reagan administrations brought with it serious consequences for the acid rain issue, so did the change from the Reagan to the Bush administrations. Indeed, candidate George Bush promised that if he were elected, the environment would be a high priority (Stanfield 1988, 1510). Immediately after taking office, he pledged to a joint session of Congress that he would soon introduce legislation to reduce acid rain *(New York Times* 1989, A17). The very day after his speech to Congress, Bush traveled to Canada, where he repeated his promise to Prime Minister Mulroney and the Canadian people (Dowd 1989, A3). True to his word, Bush officially proposed acid rain legislation to Congress on June 12, 1989.

The optimism generated by the Bush initiative was reflected in headlines that read, "Bush Pledge Is Breath of Fresh Air for Environmentalists" (Diemer 1989, A1) and "Clean Air Backers Like Way Wind Is Blowing" (Shabecoff 1989, B6). Survey and interview results of key participants directly involved in the acid rain debate in both the United States and Canada during the summer of 1989 also reflected that optimism; an overwhelming majority of the respondents reported that the change from Reagan to Bush would bring about (or had brought about) a major shift toward making acid rain a more prominent policy issue (Alm 1993, 26–27).[4] This optimism proved correct. While it took more than a year and a half from Bush's initial proposal, acid rain legislation was passed in November of 1990.

Although the importance of finally having a president who supported acid rain legislation should not be underestimated, a series of events actually prompted the passage of legislation.[5] Not only did President Bush support legislation, but—because a compromise on motor vehicle emissions had been reached—there was a marked quieting of the rhetoric and opposition from John Dingell, which had been so divisive in this debate (Hager 1989b, 2621). In addition, the Senate had a new majority leader (George Mitchell of Maine) who supported acid rain controls, the White House had a new chief of staff (John Sununu, former Governor of New Hampshire) who had worked for controls in the past, and the EPA had an administrator (William Riley) with a strong environmental background. These changes, all occurring over the same brief time span (from 1988 to 1990) appear to have been instrumental in final passage of acid rain legislation.[6]

The policy debate in the United States over acid rain ended with the passage of the Clean Air Act Amendments in November of 1990. President George Bush called these Amendments "the most significant air pollution legislation in our nation's history" (*EPA Journal* 1991, 1) and EPA administrator William Reilly stated that the promise made by the United States Congress in its passage of the 1970 Clean Air Act "[was] finally back on the path to fulfillment" (1991, 2). Title IV of the 1990 Clean Air Act Amendments, appropriately labeled "Acid Deposition Control," mandated large decreases in the two major precursors of acid rain: a 10-million-ton reduction of sulfur dioxide emissions (beginning in 1995) and a 2-million-ton reduction in nitrogen oxide emissions (beginning in 2000).

The provisions of the 1990 Clean Air Act Amendments (and the United States intentions to implement them in a timely manner) were confirmed when the United States and Canada signed the Air Quality Accord in March of 1991. In fact, Annex 1 of the Air Quality Accord essentially restated the mandates (as described above) of reducing emissions as they were delineated in the United States Clean Air Act Amendments.[7] Seemingly, the Canadian efforts to get the United States to act resulted in a specific United States policy to do what the Canadians had been asking for nearly a decade: reduce the amount of acid rain–causing emissions in the United States. [These efforts by the Canadians to get the United States to act in a timely manner to reduce cross-border pollution are the subject of the next chapter.]

ACID RAIN AS A WIDER POLICY PROBLEM

It would be incomplete and inaccurate to describe the acid rain issue as solely within the confines of presidential and congressional prerogatives. The scope of the issue reached far beyond the Washington beltway. Certainly President Reagan's intransigence, coupled with the opposition from Robert Byrd in the Senate and John Dingell in the House, were major deterrents to bringing about acid rain controls. Nonetheless, many other factors played a role in keeping acid rain legislation from moving forward.

The attempt to produce a domestic acid rain policy in the United States meant dealing with interregional conflicts set within a framework defined by economic and energy demands (coal production) as well as environmental and health concerns. The debate involved the complications arising from the gross inequities created by the regional location of high-sulfur coals and low-sulfur coals, questions of how pollution reduction policy would be funded, the lack of a truly accepted scientific consensus on a practical solution, and a debate at the bilateral level between the United States and Canada. The next few sections will briefly discuss several of the controversies that swirled around the acid rain issue and kept the policy debate lively and indeterminate.

Economic and Energy Concerns

Early in the subsequent legislative deliberations, two factions with opposing viewpoints emerged. Each of these factions sought to redefine acid rain policy proposals along economic lines. Proponents of governmental control argued that acid rain damage would result in the loss of thousands of jobs in the tourist industry and millions of dollars in the sport-fishing industry (U.S. Congress. Senate. Committee on Environment and Public Works 1980, 2). On the other hand, opponents of governmental intervention contended that imposing additional controls on acid rain would mean the loss of thousands of coal mining jobs (U.S. Congress. Senate. Committee on Energy and Natural Resources, Subcommittee on Energy Regulation 1980, 62–63) and huge increases in the cost of electricity to consumers (U.S. Congressional Research Service 1982, 1–3). As time passed, the acid rain issue became increasingly embedded in the politics of cost-benefit analysis (Regens and Rycroft 1988, 85–111).

An analysis of the acid rain bills proposed in Congress throughout the 1980s by several government entities indicated that the money involved in solving the acid rain problem would be truly substantial. The Office of Technology Assessment (OTA) completed a study in June, 1984 that concluded that the cost of legislative proposals to control acid deposition at that time would be $3–6 billion per year. Furthermore, OTA projected an increase in the total cost of environmental regulations by 5–10 percent and a rise in average electricity costs amounting to 4–5 percent, with increases as high as 10–15 percent in several states (U.S. Office of Technology Assessment 1984, 8–21).

Additional evidence for this view was offered in a report by the General Accounting Office (GAO), which estimated the cost of two acid rain bills at $5.4 billion and $6.9 billion per year (U.S. General Accounting Office 1984, 91). In addition, a Congressional Research Service (CRS) study concluded that the major Senate proposal was likely to cost $8.7–9.4 billion per year (U.S. Congressional Research Service 1987b, 4). Initial estimates for President Bush's 1989 acid rain proposal ranged from $14 to $18 billion per year (Stevenson 1989, D1) and final estimates of full implementation of the 1990 Clean Air Act Amendments by the year 2005 were in the range of $25 billion per year (Rosenberg 1991, 5).

It should be noted that these were the costs of acting. But what about the costs of not acting? In other words, what were the estimated costs of damage resulting from acid rain? There were relatively few analyses of the actual damage caused by acid rain (or of the benefits of controls). However, the extant literature at the time suggested that the probable fiscal impacts would be quite high. The CRS published the results of benefit-estimate studies that had been completed through 1987, which included a report that estimated a $2-billion per year cost from acid deposition upon galvanized steel, paint, and stone in the 17 northeastern states (U.S. Congressional Research Service 1987b, 47).

A more widely cited damage estimate by Thomas Crocker put the cost of acid precipitation effects on existing economic activities in the eastern third of the United States at close to $5 billion per year (U.S. Congress. Senate.

Committee on Environment and Public Works 1980, 100). Others considered this a conservative estimate. Orie Loucks, science director of the Institute of Ecology, argued that Crocker understated the true costs and that they were actually closer to $6–12 billion per year (U.S. Congress. Senate. Committee on Environment and Public Works 1980, 144). [A discussion of the long-term costs as they relate to possible environmental damage appears later in this chapter.]

Another measure of the scope of the acid rain issue was the amount of research produced and its cost. During the 1980s alone, hundreds of scientific studies were presented to Congress by various agencies.[8] Most of this research was sponsored by five agencies (the Department of Energy [DOE], the Department of Interior [DOI], the Environmental Protection Agency [EPA], the National Oceanic and Atmospheric Administration [NOAA], and the Department of Agriculture [USDA]). In 1987, the General Accounting Office reported that a total of more than $300 million had been spent on research through fiscal year 1987 alone, and that there were no plans to reduce funding in the near future (U.S. General Accounting Office 1987, 11).[9]

As mentioned earlier, economic survival and loss of jobs were two highly publicized topics of discussion. The adverse reaction to President Bush's original proposal, expressed by representatives of affected groups, indicated concern about employment-related consequences. Richard Trumpka, president of the United Mine Workers of America, claimed that if Bush's proposal became law, over 30,000 coal mining and related jobs would be lost throughout the United States, with certain areas of the Midwest and Appalachia becoming economic ghost regions (Victor 1989, 1990). Governor Celeste of Ohio estimated losses of 10,000 to 12,000 jobs in southeastern Ohio if acid rain legislation were passed (Gerdel 1989, C1). These fears were not new. Earlier proposals had generated nationwide estimates of job losses ranging up to 80,000 for the mining industry (Mosher 1983b, 1591).

Money was also linked to the total number of people affected by the acid rain issue by a critical political question: who would pay the cost of program development? If, as indicated by OTA, average electric bills were to rise 4–5 percent across the United States, the impact on most United States taxpayers would be far from negligible. One of the major reasons that federal legislators from the West and South were generally opposed to a large-scale program was their desire not to pay for what they perceived as an eastern problem. Moreover, distributing the costs across all United States citizens was objectionable to some, since an action of this sort would violate the "polluter pays" principle and present an unwarranted subsidy to residents of the Midwest.

In addition, both opponents and advocates of acid rain policy proposals were more than willing to play upon public fears—particularly as they related to energy consumption—to bolster their respective positions. For example, a particularly useful ploy of coal and utility interests lobbying against costly abatement programs lay in communicating the possibility of domination by foreign oil interests. The main contention of these interests was that higher regulatory compliance costs would effectively slow the consumption of coal as a domestic fuel source. This, in turn, would continue a pattern of overreliance on imported oil to meet consumer and industry demand (Carroll 1986, 260–61). Not all arguments, though, were related to economic costs and energy concerns alone. Health costs were also part of the discussion.

Health Concerns

At the outset of the acid rain debate, the focus was on lakes, streams, and the threat acidic compounds posed to certain fish species. Later, although there remained considerable disagreement, some scientists raised serious concerns about the impact of acid rain on human health, while others insisted that even with the best pollution controls in place, human health would be adversely affected (Koch 1980b, 1488; Likens 1976, 33).

Proponents of a regulatory solution tended to emphasize the possibility of harm. In 1987, Senator George Mitchell warned of the possible long-term adverse health effects of acid rain on the children of North America (U.S. Congress. Senate. Committee on Environment and Public Works, Subcommittee on Environmental Protection 1987, 1). Witnesses appearing before congressional committee hearings indicated that sulfates might be responsible for over 185,000 premature deaths from respiratory disease each year in the United States (U.S. Congress. House of Representatives. Committee on Interstate and Foreign Commerce, Subcommittee on Oversight and Investigations 1980, 406) and cited research suggesting a link between higher levels of air pollution and hospital admissions of children (U.S. Congress. Senate. Committee on Environment and Public Works, Subcommittee on Environmental Protection 1987, 4). Despite the enduring complaints of those who argued that human health was not an issue in this debate, the proponents of acid rain control were successful in keeping the question of health at the forefront of their position.

The above discussion reveals how acid rain was expanded from a strictly environmental issue to include economic, energy, and health concerns. It is also readily apparent, when reading about the various aspects of the acid rain debate, that regional issues continued to play a major part in the acid rain policy formulation, discussion, and conflict.

Regionalism

The policy debate over the acid rain issue that led to the passage of the 1990 Clean Air Act Amendments offers a study in regional conflict and highlights the part that regionalism can and does play in national environmental policy making. One reporter spoke of "the seething regional dispute over acid rain [as] open warfare on Capitol Hill" (Koch 1980a, 1486) and another reporter submitted that "acid rain politics are sometimes partisan—but always regional" (J. Davis 1984, 622). Some scholars have even argued that no other environmental controversy in recent times has so divided the nation along such definable regional lines (Crandall 1984, 21; Gould 1985, 55–62; R. Meyer and Yandle 1987, 527–36; Regens and Rycroft 1988, 129–32).

The early acid rain debate was centered almost exclusively in the eastern portion of the United States. At its simplest level, the debate was defined as a problem of property rights: a classic two-party externality struggle wherein the highly valued production of electricity in coal-fired utilities in the Ohio River Valley began a process that led to the deposition of acid rain on valuable resources in the Northeast (R. Meyer and Yandle 1987, 527).

On another level, there was an obvious difference of intensity in interest between the eastern and western states with respect to the acid rain issue. Throughout the 1980s, the major lawsuits involving acid rain all came from the eastern states (Schmandt, Clarkson, and Roderick 1988, 230). In addition, the five states that passed their own acid rain legislation were all from the eastern part of the United States (Mangun 1995, 43–44). During this same period of time, the major government reports and analyses on acid rain set up a clear regional distinction between states east and west of the Mississippi. The Office of Technology Assessment, the General Accounting Office, the Congressional Research Service, and the National Acid Precipitation Assessment Program all delineated two major geographical regions of concern in terms of acid rain: the 31 easternmost states bordering and east of the Mississippi River and the rest of the states west of the Mississippi.

The idea was transmitted that this was an eastern problem that in some way or form should be solved by easterners. In his acid rain proposal, chairperson of the Senate Committee on the Environment and Public Works, Quentin Burdick (Democrat from North Dakota), summed up this feeling by arguing that the United States must "clean up things east of the Mississippi first, then take care of the rest of the country afterward" (Stern 1986, 2829). This idea, as well as the distinction between the regions east and west of the Mississippi River, were also used in some form by political scientists who analyzed the acid rain debate (Gould 1985; Kahan 1986; Regens and Rycroft 1988). Many of the bills introduced in Congress recognized this distinction, and the final acid rain law, passed in the winter of 1990, included language that granted special considerations to states in the eastern United States.

In reality, though, the acid rain issue was expanded from concern for 200 lakes in the Adirondacks (U.S. Congress. House of Representatives. Committee on Interstate and Foreign Commerce, Subcommittee on Energy and Power 1980, 222) to concern for 20,000 lakes nationwide (U.S. Congress. Senate. Committee on Foreign Relations, Subcommittee on Arms Control, Oceans, International Operations and Environment 1982, 31). In addition, a 1988 Environmental Defense Fund study linked acid rain to the deterioration of coastal waters in the Chesapeake Bay area (U.S. Congress. Senate. Committee on Commerce, Science, and Transportation 1988, 1–6). Other studies indicated that acid rain affected all regions of the United States, including the West (Roth et al. 1985, 1–11), Southwest (LaFranchi 1987, 6), and Southeast (Shabicoff 1988, A1). Even though regionalism was in the forefront of the acid rain issue, the reality was that acid rain was more than a regional issue. And the unknown long-term effects of acid rain complicated the issue even more.

The Complexity of the Acid Rain Issue

There is little doubt that the acid rain issue was characterized as fairly complex by the public, policy makers, and scientists who dealt with acid rain on a daily basis (Alm and C. Davis 1993, 811–13). As seen in the discussion in the presidential/congressional section of this chapter, the causes and effects of acid rain were not clear-cut. What was lacking was a truly accepted scientific consensus about acid rain. Was it really a problem? What caused acid rain? Were the effects of acid rain damaging enough to need expensive reduction programs? What would happen if there was a delay in implementing programs until science and scientists could produce more answers?

An understanding of the complexity of the issue can be obtained by examining the extent and nature of scientists' involvement in policy making, especially in terms of gathering and disseminating information. One rather simple indicator of the extent of their involvement is the number of times they were called on to testify at the congressional hearings involving acid rain. Data gathered from hearings during the 1980s indicate that scientists were active participants, with the greatest amount of their testimony given during the early part of the decade.[10] Overall, scientists constituted at least 12 percent of the total number of witnesses (160/1319). If the scientists who testified as representatives of state and federal agencies are included, the rate climbs as high as 34 percent (444/1319). Much of the scientific testimony was provided by university researchers such as Ellis Cowling of North Carolina State (who testified 9 times) and James Galloway of the University of Virginia (who testified 5 times).

Scientific complexity was also illustrated by agreement (or disagreement) over the causes and effects of acid rain. A review of the literature has revealed that despite the fact that several major scientific studies by the National Academy of Sciences, the Office of Technology Assessment, and the Office of Science and Technology Policy, concluded that available scientific evidence justified immediate action to control acid rain, many of the representatives in Congress wanted a much stronger scientific consensus prior to consideration of policy proposals (U.S. Congress. House of Representatives. Committee on Science and Technology, Subcommittee on Natural Resources, Agricultural Research and Environment 1981, 489). EPA administrators Gorsuch, Ruckelshaus, and Thomas also expressed this position. In testimony before the United States Congress, each one of these administrators unequivocally expressed serious doubts that the basic scientific and technical issues concerning acid rain would soon be resolved (U.S. Congress. House of Representatives. Committee on Energy and Commerce, Subcommittee on Health and the Environment 1982, 285; U.S. Congress. House of Representatives. Committee on Science and Technology 1984, 16; U.S. Congress. Senate. Committee on Energy and Natural Resources 1986, 91). Furthermore, they all voiced the opinion (representative of President Reagan's long established belief) that no scientific consensus existed to justify immediate action to control acid rain pollution.

In 1985, Sandra Postel wrote that "[d]estruction caused by acid rain and air pollution two decades from now may dwarf that evident today" (1985, 115). This statement reflects one of the most controversial aspects of acid rain: the possible irreversibility of its damage.   Despite the scientific uncertainty involved, many proponents of acid rain control based their argument for immediate action on the belief that the adverse environmental impacts associated with acid rain were long-term and irreversible (S. Brown 1981, 634; Harsha 1983, 19).

An impressive chain of circumstantial evidence had convinced a large number of United States citizens that a genuine threat of widespread irreversible environmental damage existed (Kahan 1986, ii). This belief was picked up and faithfully reiterated by proponents of acid rain controls.   A review of the introductory remarks typically offered at congressional hearings on acid rain reveals the popularity of phrases such as the "potentially catastrophic dimensions" of irreversible damage (U.S. Congress. House of Representatives. Committee on Interstate and Foreign Commerce, Subcommittee on Oversight and Investigations 1980, 1).

Compounding the prospect of irreversible damage was the long lead time required to put an acid rain reduction program into effect. OTA estimated that it would require a minimum of 7 to 10 years to implement a program to reduce emissions significantly (U.S. Office of Technology Assessment 1984, 9). Over the years, the bills proposed in the Congress indicated a clear recognition by policy makers of the time frame needed to institute an acid rain program.   In 1983, the major bill in the House (HR 3400) requested enactment by 1993 and the two major bills in the Senate (S768 and S769) requested enactment by 1994 and 1998, respectively.   OTA's initial time estimates turned out to be fairly accurate.   The 1990 Clean Air Act Amendments called for a two-phased, market-based system to reduce sulfur dioxide emissions from power plants by half: Phase I was to be complete by the year 1995 and phase II was to commence in the year 2000, with a goal of complete implementation by the year 2005.

The call to establish a sound, scientific data base on which to make decisions was a further complication. Dr. Gene Likens of Cornell University, who had been studying the effects of acid rain for over twenty years, argued that short-term measurements (3 to 5 years) might be misleading and that decades are required to detect actual biogeochemical trends in complex ecosystems (1989, 173).   Likens' research was based on data collected from the only long-term monitoring station in the United States, Hubbard Brook Experimental Forest in New Hampshire, where research was initiated in 1963 (Driscoll et al. 1989, 137). This need for additional long-term monitoring data, coupled with the lead time necessary to institute a reduction program, reflected a time frame of resolution extending well into the next century.

As if the acid rain issue were not complex enough, it was believed by some investigators that acid rain is also closely associated with other pollutants. Early in the debate, two researchers at the National Center for Atmospheric Research (Steven Rhodes and Paulette Middleton) complained that acid rain was being treated in the policy-making arena "as though it [was] unrelated to visibility and other air quality issues—despite the commonality of responsible pollutants" (Rhodes and Middleton 1983a, 35). These investigators went on to document how closely acid rain was related to what they considered the four key pollutants: sulfur dioxide, nitrogen oxides, volatile organic compounds, and fine particulate matter. In essence, they concluded that acid rain was not a novel problem caused by a new pollutant but only the latest environmental insult associated with these four established pollutants.

Rhodes' and Middleton's conclusions found support among other researchers and scientists. Sandra Postel maintained that publicity focused primarily on acid rain tended to ignore its interrelationships with other pollutants such as ozone and carbon dioxide (1985, 101), and James Galloway stressed the need to deal with acid rain within the context of a holistic view of what sensitive ecosystems receive from the atmosphere (U.S. Congress. Senate. Committee on Environment and Public Works 1986, 449).[11]

POSSIBLE SOLUTIONS

In 1984, OTA released a comprehensive report entitled *Acid Rain and Transported Air Pollutants: Implications for Public Policy*. Although the recommendations of this report went unheeded at the time, the report did provide an analysis of the major policy options available to deal with acid rain. Two options received the most governmental attention: (1) mandating emissions reductions to further control the primary sources of transported pollutants and (2) modifying the federal acid deposition research program to provide more timely guidance for congressional decisions (U.S. Office of Technology Assessment 1984, 22–34). Whereas the first option called for controls, the second option called for more study.

From the very beginning, technological uncertainty surrounded the acid rain issue. Unresolved scientific questions included which pollutants should be controlled (Rhodes and Middleton 1983a, 32–35), what level of pollution control should be required (Jeffrey Smith 1981, 770), whether local or transported pollutants presented the greatest danger (Kerr 1982, 881), whether there was a linear relationship between emissions and effects (U.S. Congress. House of Representatives. Committee on Science and Technology, Subcommittee on Natural Resources, Agricultural Research and Environment 1981, 186), and how much time it would take to correct the problem (LaBastille 1981, 673). Yet, according to the leading authorities, the technology was already present to reduce acid rain. The answer was flue-gas desulfurization (commonly called "scrubbers"), which had proven to reduce sulfur emissions by 90 to 95 percent and nitrogen oxide emissions by 50 percent (U.S. National Acid Precipitation Assessment Program 1987, 39). Scrubbers were considered the most technologically advanced method for reducing emissions of sulfur-bearing particles from coal-fired power plants.[12]

However, no matter how successful scrubbers were technologically, their implementation faced economic and political obstacles. Retrofitting coal-burning facilities with scrubbers is extremely expensive, costing the utility industry billions of dollars per year (Navarro 1981, 135–42). These high costs inhibited the acceptance of scrubbers as a way to reduce emissions, especially since no generally accepted scientific studies were available that quantified the benefits of pollution reduction in terms agreeable to those in power.

Furthermore, a tremendous amount of resentment existed among western policy makers over what they perceived as a misuse of technology in writing the Clean Air Act Amendments of 1977 to force the use of scrubbers on new plants. Utility operators in the Rocky Mountain West believed that they could meet the clean-air standards by burning low-sulfur coal—which was plentiful in their geographical area—without the use of scrubbers. Moreover, they believed the only reason scrubbers were mandated was to protect high-sulfur-coal mining jobs in Appalachia and the Midwest. Senator Alan Simpson (Democrat, Wyoming) stated that "We in the West have long memories [of how the 1977 Clean Air Act Amendments] gimmicked the nation's coal markets so that high-sulfur coal would have an advantage over low-sulfur in the marketplace" (J. Davis 1988, 2812). Senator Simpson vowed that it would never happen again.

Other options, like coal-scrubbing, were met with just as much resistance as the use of scrubbers, because they were believed to incur unacceptably high economic costs in terms of transportation, retrofitting, and the loss of coal mining jobs in certain regions of the country (U.S. General Accounting Office 1984, 77–109). Even the highly promising Clean Coal Technology Program, initiated by the Department of Energy and advanced by several top American scientists as yielding the most environmentally and economically attractive solution to the acid rain problem, was viewed as a long-term program unlikely to yield results any time in the immediate future (Mohnen 1988, 30–38; U.S. Congressional Research Service 1987a, 1–29).

The solution ultimately agreed upon, as specified in the 1990 Clean Air Act Amendments, did not mandate the use of scrubbers or any technology-forcing means. Instead, the solution was based on using marketplace inducements, with the goal of cutting emissions in half by the turn of the century. A two-phased market system was set up to reduce sulfur dioxide emissions by 10 million tons (from 1980 levels) by the year 2000.[13] An acid rain emissions trading program was established whereby utility plants were issued allowances based on fixed emission rates set by law and based on previous fossil-fuel use. Utilities pay penalties if emissions exceed their allowances, but allowances can be banked and traded.

Title IV of the 1990 Clean Air Act Amendments also allocated 50,000 extra allowances per year to plants in ten midwestern states, and these allowances were not subject to the 8.9-million ton cap on emissions. Additionally, Title IV authorized 50 million dollars to provide need-based payments, training, and employment services to workers (e.g., coal miners in the Midwest) laid off or fired as a result of employers' compliance with the Clean Air Act. Because of these exceptions and the unproven worth of the market mechanisms, considerable skepticism still exists as to whether this solution will ultimately be economically or politically successful.[14]

SUMMARY

Early in the policy debate, the acid rain issue was restricted in several ways. First, acid rain was a matter of concern only to a few highly specialized researchers and scientists rather than to policy makers or the United States public. Second, acid rain was narrowly defined, in environmental terms alone. Third, there was no apparent crisis or focusing event to bring the acid rain issue onto the governmental agenda. However, as time went by, the acid rain issue was expanded to include a larger and larger group of actors and redefined to cover a much broader scope of interests, including economic, energy, and health concerns. Eventually, acid rain became a relevant problem on the governmental agenda.

Despite consistent opposition from the Reagan Administration, support for acid rain proposals evolved into a bipartisan issue. Even though President Reagan, a Republican, was accurately portrayed as a significant hurdle to the development of corrective legislation, the two individuals in Congress widely considered to be the primary blockers were Senator Robert Byrd of West Virginia and Representative John Dingell of Michigan, both Democrats. Indeed, conflict between political parties was less pronounced than differences between regions of the country.

As is apparent from examining the primary blockers in Congress, the acid rain issue was delineated within the context of regional interests. The Northeast was perceived as the victim of pollution originating in midwestern states. Elected officials from the Midwest ardently opposed abatement proposals based on the "polluter pays" principle, while western legislators became equally adamant in their position that proposals aimed at distributing program development costs throughout the United States constituted an unjustified subsidy to pollution-generating firms and consumers within a relatively small cluster of states.

There was a vast amount of scientific testimony given at congressional hearings, and hundreds of scientific reports attempting to explain the causes and effects of acid rain were presented to Congress. The prominence and frequency of expert scientific testimony, as well as the large number of government organizations dealing with this issue, served to highlight the level of official concern over the complexities and uncertainties of the scientific debate. Don Munton summarized the impact of science as follows:

Absent the new scientific evidence . . . opponents of acid rain controls in the United States would have maintained the upper hand and would have much more strenuously and successfully resisted controls. . . . There was a slow change of thinking amongst Americans on acid rain brought about by the mounting scientific evidence and increasing calls for action. Those who were advocating controls in the early 1980s were steadily joined by more and more supporters. Cumulation of scientific research and the continuing movement toward adoption of control policies by other governments made it increasingly untenable to argue against the need for acid rain controls in the United States or against bearing the costs. (1997b, 22–23)

The final passage of acid rain legislation suggests that through the political process, the difficulties of weighing all the options were overcome, the scientific uncertainties dealt with, and a coherent and comprehensive policy to reduce the emissions that lead to acid rain was developed. However, the author would be remiss not to examine the role that Canada played in the formulation of the United States acid rain policy. Hence, before this story moves to a direct analysis of the science of acid rain, the next chapter will highlight the efforts of the Canadians to bring about change in the United States.

NOTES

1. By the time the lawsuit reached the Washington, D.C. Circuit Court, President Reagan was in office and the Court reaffirmed the Reagan administration's decision to wait for definitive evidence of acid rain damage before limiting emissions.

2. President Reagan gave ample notice through campaign speeches in 1980 and through subsequent political appointments that ecological goals would be subordinated to economic goals (Vig and Kraft 1984, 22–23). Getting government off the backs of business by cutting back or even eliminating regulatory activities fell disproportionately on the shoulders of administrators in charge of environmental and consumer protection programs. President Reagan's policy priorities were sufficiently disconcerting to members of Congress more closely tied to environmental policy goals that they created a new form of deferral politics, effectively postponing the introduction of new regulatory programs until a more favorable political climate for their consideration was in place (Cook and Davidson 1985, 47–76).

3. A September, 1980 Harris Poll revealed overwhelming support for continuing the nation's clean-up of its air and for the Clean Air Act as it was currently written. A majority of 51 percent wanted to keep the statute as it was; another 29 percent wanted to make it tougher; and only 17 percent wanted to relax it (Mosher 1981b, 1996).

4. As documented in Chapter 1, the author carried out a survey of 139 people (return rate of 62%) and interviews of 51 people. The people selected for the interviews and surveys were involved in the acid rain debate in both the United States and Canada and had either directly or indirectly participated in congressional hearings involving acid rain. Respondents and interviewees included congressional staff members from the House and Senate, representatives of the utility and coal industries, leaders of environmental groups, members of government agencies, and researchers and scientists.

5. With headlines that read "The 'White House Effect' Opens a Long-Locked Political Door" (Hager 1990, 139) and "Bush Makes the Difference" (Pytte 1990, 3587), it is easy to see why many people perceived Bush as the key player in bringing about acid rain legislation.

6. For a more detailed analysis of these changes see Simon and Alm (1995).

7. Alan Schwartz observed that "it could be convincingly argued that in order to get an agreement whereby the U.S. would commit to significant progress on the issue of acid

rain, Canada accepted using the U.S. CAA as a basis for a bilateral agreement" (1994, 501).

8. Sharon Begley and Mary Hager reported in an article in *Newsweek* that as of August, 1986, over "3000 scientific papers and seven major government reports have weighed in on the causes and effects of acid rain" (1986, 53). Also, in 1987, NAPAP reported that it had supported over 1000 scientific publications on acid rain (U.S. National Acid Precipitation Assessment Program 1987, 2).

9. Indeed, by 1991 the total amount spent by NAPAP was estimated at $530 million (Cowling 1992, 111).

10. These numbers were generated by the author from the hearings held in Congress on acid rain from 1979 through 1990.

11. According to many scientists, the conviction that the acid rain phenomenon is ultimately linked to a host of other air-related issues of a global nature, such as climate change, stratospheric ozone depletion, and the long-range transport of atmospheric pollutants, remains strong within the scientific community today (Gorham 1996, 109; Schindler et al. 1996, 705; Yan et al. 1996, 141).

12. A good description of exactly how a scrubber works is provided by Ackerman and Hassler (1981, 14–17).

13. Reductions in nitrogen oxide (the other major precursor of acid rain pollution) were to be achieved through performance standards set by EPA.

14. As of today, the trading system has received generally good reviews. See U.S. Environmental Protection Agency (1998) and Ringquist (1998).

Chapter 3

Canada and the United States Acid Rain Debate

INTRODUCTION

Chapter 2 provided a description of the acid rain debate as it played out in the United States from the late 1970s through the early 1990s (when, in 1990 legislation was finally passed and signed into law by the president). One aspect of the acid rain policy debate in the United States that was mentioned (but not emphasized) was the part that Canada played in keeping the United States focused on reducing acid rain pollution. This chapter describes the Canadian involvement.

It must be remembered that only 3 months after the 1990 Clean Air Act Amendments were signed into law, the United States signed an agreement with Canada (the Air Quality Accord) stating its intention to reduce cross-border pollution. This agreement is touted as a guarantee of cleaner air and a healthier environment for millions of Canadians and Americans. Indeed, the Accord is viewed as the beginning of a new era of environmental cooperation between the United States and Canada (U.S. Environmental Protection Agency 1994, 5). If this is true, the signing of the Accord ended more than a decade of what Don Munton called "one of the more contentious issues in Canadian-American relations" (1983, 13).

It must also be remembered that at the very beginning of the United States policy debate over acid rain, the Canadians claimed that it was their duty to "raise the level of appreciation" in the United States of the consequences of acid rain pollution (U.S. Congress. House of Representatives. Committee on Science and Technology, Subcommittee on Natural Resources, Agricultural Research and Environment 1981, 433). Canadians did just that, and they did more. They helped define and frame the acid rain issue as both an environmental and cross-border concern that the United States needed to address. Canadians were also (at least partially) responsible for maintaining the acid rain issue on the United States governmental agenda and for helping to open the policy window that led to a formal United States policy to reduce acid rain pollution.

The following sections are designed to provide the reader with an overview of this Canadian effort to influence the direction of the United States policy debate over acid rain. This overview will also help in establishing a framework for analyzing the beliefs of both United States and Canadian scientists about science and environmental policy making.[1]

CANADIAN EFFORTS: THE EARLY 1980s

As you may recall, negotiations over acid rain policy officially began between Canada and the United States in the late 1970s, after the release of a bilateral Canada–United States report that estimated that the United States was producing 70 to 80 percent of the transboundary air pollution. Groups in both countries demanded some sort of bilateral negotiations. In Canada, the movement toward negotiations was initially led by Environment Minister LeBlanc, who argued that the acid rain problem in Canada (which he dramatically called "an environmental time bomb") could not be solved without action on the part of the United States (Munton 1980–81, 165–66). In the United States, it was a small group of congressmen from states that bordered Canada that fostered a resolution from Congress calling for the president to open negotiations with Canada to reduce cross-border pollution (J. Johnson 1985, 268; U.S. General Accounting Office 1981, 43).

In 1979, President Jimmy Carter responded to this call for negotiations by pledging funding for an acid rain study (*CQ Almanac* 1979, 603). Shortly thereafter (in 1980), two events signaled that acid rain was to become a primary concern of policy makers in both the United States and Canada. First, Congress mandated a 10–year scientific, economic, and technological study to examine the causes and effects of acid rain. This study was authorized under the Acid Precipitation Act of 1980 and coordinated by an interagency task force consisting of representatives of twelve federal agencies and four national laboratories, together with four presidential appointees. The actual work was carried out under the auspices of the National Acid Precipitation Assessment Program.

Second, the United States and Canada signed the *Memorandum of Intent Concerning Transboundary Air Pollution* (MOI). Among other actions, the MOI established a Canada–United States Coordinating Committee, an exchange of scientific information, and a promise to promote vigorous enforcement of existing laws and regulations in order to limit emissions from new and existing facilities, with the goal of reducing transboundary air pollution (U.S. Department of State 1980, 1–4).

Canada's initial response was to view acid rain as a bilateral environmental problem to be solved solely through diplomatic channels.[2] Canada's tack was to use negotiations at the State Department level to achieve a bilateral agreement that would reduce the flow of acid pollutants between the countries. The principal actors were very optimistic that this route would be successful. However, when Ronald Reagan replaced Jimmy Carter as president of the United States in January of 1981, the nature of the cooperative efforts between the two nations changed. It did not take the Canadians very long to realize that the newly elected Reagan administration had no intention of vigorously enforcing environmental laws or of taking any action to reduce cross-border pollution. Shortly after the signing of the MOI, Canadians found themselves expressing grave concerns over the pace of progress and officially denounced the Reagan administration for refusing to move forward on the acid rain issue (Sullivan 1987, 10).

Canadians responded to the Reagan administration's failure to act in a manner that did not hide their intentions or strategy.[3] A report by the Subcommittee on Acid Rain of the Canadian Parliament in 1981 titled *Still Waters* plainly outlined the commitment that the Canadians adopted. While not abandoning the ultimate goal of reaching a bilateral agreement with the United States, the Canadians clearly moved far beyond diplomatic negotiations. Among other things, the subcommittee recommended that:

Governments, public interest groups, and individual Canadians in general explore and utilize all possible political, legal, administrative and media channels to ensure that acid rain–causing emissions originating in the United States are substantially reduced;

the acid rain problem and its transboundary implications be publicized and discussed at appropriate meetings of the International Parliamentary Associations . . . [particularly] . . . the annual meetings of the Canada–United States Inter-parliamentary Group;

Environment Canada . . . expand its public awareness and information program on acid rain to alert and educate the Canadian public;

a major public awareness and information program is necessary to generate public concern in the United States about the acid rain problem and the threat it poses to the Canadian and American environments. . . . Consideration should be given to inviting influential American media representatives to Canada so they can be apprised of the transboundary effects of U.S.–sourced air pollution. (Canada. House of Commons. Committee on Fisheries and Forests, Subcommittee on Acid Rain 1981, 94–100)

Furthermore, it was clear that the Canadian effort was going to go far beyond official government response. The Canadian Coalition on Acid Rain (CCAR) publicly announced that Canadians could not depend on their government to persuade United States officials to solve the acid rain problem. Members of the CCAR also proclaimed that it would take "a powerful, organized effort in the United States by Canadian citizens" to bring about success (Canada. House of Commons. Committee on Fisheries and Forests, Subcommittee on Acid Rain 1981, 94). This effort would include hiring United States legal counsel, retaining United States lobbyists, and organizing to help draft legislation, promote litigation, and put pressure on the White House, Congress, and the American people. As Everett Cataldo explained, the Canadians realized that they "[might] have a better chance of negotiating a settlement with the United States by attempting to influence U.S. domestic policy decisions, than [by] signing a formal treaty" (1992, 396).

Members of CCAR and Canadian government officials enthusiastically adopted the strategy delineated above and became outspoken public participants in the acid rain debate (Mosher 1981a, 1301). They distributed "Stop Acid Rain" material to tourists (Clarkson 1983, 14), sent members of their parliament and embassy to the United States to conduct workshops and seminars on acid rain (Mosher 1983a, 999), established the first registered Canadian lobby in the United States to work for a nongovernment, nonbusiness citizen's organization (Carroll 1982, 43), and distributed two controversial films about acid rain to interested groups and individuals in the United States, including members of Congress (J. Davis 1982a, 1347).[4]

In addition, members of the Canadian government did something that was unthinkable before this time; they provided in-person testimony to the United States Congress. At the first hearing the United States held on acid rain, the Canadians (led by the Environmental Counselor of the Canadian Embassy, George Rejhon) had politely declined to testify in person.[5] Soon, however, this view drastically changed. Over the next year and a half, over a dozen Canadian representatives, including members of the Canadian Embassy and Canadian Parliament, testified at United States hearings on acid rain. One of the very first scientific reports introduced into the United States Congress was a report about the effects of acid rain on the Canadian ecosystem, which was prepared by the Canadian Embassy (U.S. Congress. House of Representatives. Committee on Interstate and Foreign Commerce, Subcommittee on Oversight and Investigations 1980, 5–11). In May of 1981, there was even a subcommittee hearing in Congress dedicated to the single purpose of examining Canadian claims of excessive acid rain caused by air pollutants from United States sources (U.S. Congress. House of Representatives. Committee on Foreign Affairs, Subcommittee on Human Rights and International Organizations 1981).

This Canadian testimony was a clear and deliberate departure from Canadian norms and the extreme caution with which Canada entered the debate over acid rain was reflected in the carefully-chosen words of Raymond Robinson (Canada's Assistant Deputy Minister for Environmental Protection) in his address to the United States Congress: "How the United States chooses to deal with the tradeoffs involved in addressing air or other kinds of pollution is a matter for the United States to determine. Canada has no desire to enter your domestic debate on the issue. . . . On the other hand, when your practices, both present and contemplated, threaten Canada's environmental and economic integrity, we believe we have a duty to bring our concerns to your attention" (U.S. Congress. House of Representatives. Committee on Energy and Commerce, Subcommittee on Health and the Environment 1981a, 513). Moreover, in testimony before the United States Congress, the Canadians continually emphasized the importance of listening to what both United States and Canadian scientists were saying about acid rain. George Rejhon of the Canadian Embassy summed up this view.

From your point of view as policymakers, it seems to me you have to look at the preponderance of evidence, such as comes from your National Academy of Sciences, which is overwhelming. You have to look at the distribution of the scientists who argue and how they argue in terms of where they come from and what they are saying and what are their relative numbers. If you do that, you will find that the vast majority of independent scientists basically agree with the kinds of things we have been saying today. (U.S. Congress. House of Representatives. Committee on Science and Technology, Subcommittee on Natural Resources, Agriculture Research and Environment 1981, 458–59)

After a very short period of time (covering the late 1970s and very early 1980s), the Canadians had abandoned their quiet diplomacy strategy and plunged straight into a full-fledged effort to gain public recognition in the United States, hoping it would bring about more timely action on acid rain pollution. As described by Stephen Clarkson, the Canadians had extended their diplomatic activity far beyond relations with the State Department, to the executive branch, legislature, media, special interests, and states (1983, 1). They had thrown out their traditional reactionary response to United States political developments and had done something they had long avoided, engaging themselves in the process of lobbying in America. This action was taken after considerable deliberation and only after the Canadians felt that the normal process of negotiating diplomatically had failed to secure Canadian desires. Canada clearly shifted its focus from the diplomatic route alone to targeting the entire executive branch and the legislature, as well as the public, media, and special interest groups.

CANADIAN EFFORTS: THE MID-1980s

Even though the Canadians made their greatest effort to shape the policy of another country (Clarkson 1983, 15), by the mid-1980s, the results were the same: the United States still had not developed a formal domestic or bilateral acid rain policy. Canadian interventionist public diplomacy had failed to move the United States in the desired direction and the Canadians refocused their efforts once again. There was a return to quiet diplomacy at the State Department level, a cessation of Canadian testimony at United States congressional hearings, a quieting of public rhetoric, and more important, a shift to a strategy based on traditional United States grass-roots lobbying.

Although Prime Minister Mulroney is given much of the credit for this transformation (Mulroney became the Canadian Prime Minister in 1984), indications are that the reasons for the Canadian change were much more extensive. For instance, there had been a tremendous negative reaction in the United States to some of the Canadian tactics, which, quite frankly, caught the Canadians off guard. Canadians had initially hoped that once the United States realized the tremendous consequences of its actions, it would respond to correct the problem; that the United States would do this because the Canadians wanted it done. That was not the reaction.

Those in the United States who opposed additional pollution controls (e.g., the National Coal Association and Edison Electric Institute) proved very adept at rebutting Canadian arguments and casting the Canadians in a bad light. The most frequent criticism centered upon how Canadians were dealing with the acid rain problem in their own country. The charge was leveled that Canada was asking the United States to do things that even Canada had not done. The words of William Harrison of Edison Electric Institute were typical of this point of view: "Canada should position its own environmental protection laws to be as restrictive as ours before asking us to become even more restrictive than we are at present" (U.S. Congress. Senate. Committee on Foreign Relations, Subcommittee on Arms Control, Oceans, International Operations and Environment 1982, 74).

While the Canadians argued that their sole motive was to protect their precious resources, those opposed to pollution controls argued otherwise. They pointed out that while the United States had mandatory federal standards requiring states to have federally-approved implementation plans to reduce pollution levels, Canada had no domestic plan of its own to reduce pollution levels and its federal government was essentially powerless to compel the provinces to act to reduce their pollution levels (U.S. Congress. House of Representatives. Committee on Energy and Commerce, Subcommittee on Health and the Environment 1981a, 479–80).

Opponents of change even suggested that the Canadian acid rain agenda was really part of a national conspiracy to expand Canadian sales of electrical power in the United States. For instance, James Friedman (Counsel for the Ohio Coalition on Environmental-Energy Balance) testified before Congress that he was suspicious of Canadian national energy objectives as they related to the acid rain issue because "there is a very strong economic and national self-interest stake in Canada in maximizing its position to supply bulk power to various portions of the United States" (U.S. Congress. House of Representatives. Committee on Energy and Commerce, Subcommittee on Health and the Environment 1981b, 197). More to the point, Senator Larry Pressler (Democrat, South Dakota) put it this way: "There are certain interests that suggest that the acid rain problem is a contrivance of the Canadians to sustain their nuclear power industry through electricity imports to the United States at the expense of the development of United States coal-fired power plants" (U.S. Congress. Senate. Committee on Foreign Relations, Subcommittee on Arms Control, Oceans, International Operations and Environment 1982, 71).

John Sununu, the governor of New Hampshire at the time, also had harsh words for the Canadians:

. . . and there is the public perception that has been created that our good neighbors to the north have taken up a leadership role in this issue. . . . I think there has been more lip service and less action from the north than there has been from this country. And I give you some statistics to ponder. . . . On a per capita basis, they [the Canadians] are emitting twice as much as we do, and on a per unit of industrial output basis, they are emitting three times as much as we do. If they ever achieve the 50 percent reduction that they give strong lip service to, and I have my doubts that they will even do that, and their commitment is to try and get there some time in the mid-1990s, by that time they will then only be where we as a nation are today. (U.S. Congress. Senate. Committee on Environment and Public Works 1983b, 225–26)

Despite these criticisms, the two countries continued to talk about developing a bilateral policy. As a result of these discussions, the United States and Canada signed another agreement in 1986, the *Joint Report of the Special Envoys on Acid Rain*. As mentioned earlier, the significance of this agreement was that by signing it, the Reagan administration publicly acknowledged—for the first time during the debate—that acid rain was a serious environmental problem and agreed to begin a program to control acid rain pollutants (Lewis and W. Davis 1986, 29). Yet, soon after the *Joint Report* was formalized the Reagan administration made it clear that it was not going to move very quickly to fulfill its part of the agreement (U.S. Congress. House of Representatives. Committee on Energy and Commerce, Subcommittee on Health and the Environment 1986, 223). Furthermore, congressional hearings and congressional reports reinforced the prognosis that the *Joint Report* would soon go the way of the MOI; that is, as long as Reagan remained in the United States Presidency, there would be no United States action to develop a domestic or bilateral policy to deal with the problem of acid rain pollution.

To be sure, the Canadians continued to push for action on acid rain. In an effort to show what they had accomplished and were going to accomplish, the Canadians produced scientific evidence to support their claims. But the Canadians were soon on the defensive. First, they had to admit that they were behind the United States in controlling nitrogen oxides. Prime Minister Mulroney publicly acknowledged that Canada was far behind the United States in emission controls in this significant area, and that Canada would first clean up its act before seeking stronger United States controls (U.S. Congress. Senate. Committee on Environment and Public Works 1985, 7). Even though the Canadians did exactly that and by September of 1987 had brought their automobile and light truck standards up to those of the United States (U.S. Congress. House of Representatives. Committee on Energy and Commerce, Subcommittee on Oversight and Investigations 1987, 64), the political damage had been substantial. At least for the near term, opponents of controls on the United States side constantly restated the argument that Canada had been asking the United States to correct a problem that the Canadians had not even addressed in their own country. Doubt had been cast on Canadian intentions.

The second situation that the Canadians created for themselves arose from their claim (as stated by Governor Sununu), backed by scientific evidence, that they would unilaterally reduce sulfur dioxide emissions by 50 percent by 1994. This was a bold move and showed that the Canadians were very serious indeed about cleaning up acid rain. However, this projection turned out to be technically incorrect. The anticipated reduction should have been closer to 35 percent. The primary cause of the discrepancy between these percentages was the way in which they were calculated. The 50 percent figure was calculated from a base case chosen by the Canadians rather than from actual 1980 emission levels (U.S. Congress. House of Representatives. Committee on Energy and Commerce, Subcommittee on Oversight and Investigations 1987, 64).

The Canadians reluctantly had to agree that their calculations were not made from the actual emission data. Even though Canada had a program in place to reduce their sulfur dioxide emissions by approximately 35 percent (and the United States had no program at all), the Canadians again found themselves on the defensive because it appeared that they had doctored scientific data to support their policies (U.S. Congressional Research Service 1988, 1–9). Although there was no evidence to indicate deception in the Canadian calculations, the perception was there, and the opponents of controls used this perception to question the scientific credibility of all Canadian studies related to reducing cross-border pollution.

In addition, the Canadians found themselves in an adversarial position in relation to one of the most powerful members of the United States Congress, Representative John Dingell (Democrat, Michigan) who was Chairman of the House Committee on Energy and Commerce. If acid rain legislation were to pass in the United States, it would have to go through this committee, and John Dingell was opposed to any such action. Furthermore, Dingell's environmental staff, led by David Finnegan, was generally considered the best-informed congressional staff working on clean air (R. Cohen 1995, 134). The Canadians faced a formidable opponent who did not react, but attacked.

Over the course of the debate, Dingell continually called the Canadians on the carpet. He pointed out errors in their reports, miscalculations in their scientific data, and more important, publicly chastised them for interfering in a domestic policy-making matter. Dingell even went so far as to publicly accuse the Canadians of illegal lobbying, and backed up that accusation by having both the United States State Department and Justice Department formally investigate that charge (U.S. Congress. House of Representatives. Committee on Energy and Commerce, Subcommittee on Oversight and Investigations 1987, 151–52). Although this charge was summarily dismissed, it fueled the effort to portray the Canadians as outsiders attempting to tell the United States how to run its business. These views are summed up in a letter from Dingell to Allan Gotlieb, Canadian Ambassador to the United States: "Just as I would oppose U.S. governmental officials, including legislators, lobbying within the Canadian government, so I believe that Canada's lobbying effort aimed at the Congress and our system is inappropriate. Both nations would be better served by resorting to the traditional diplomatic approach" (U.S. Congress. House of Representatives. Committee on Energy and Commerce, Subcommittee on Oversight and Investigations 1987, 78).

Whether in reaction to this harsh criticism or through the realization that the Reagan administration was never going to support acid rain controls, the Canadians (by the mid-to-late 1980s) had begun to act unilaterally to reduce acid rain pollution (Munton and Castle 1992, 325–26).[6] They committed themselves to a 50 percent reduction of acid rain pollutants by 1994 (from the 1980 levels) and renewed their strategy of quiet diplomacy at the state department level. However, the Canadians were to make one more substantial push to directly influence United States policy making regarding acid rain.

CANADIAN EFFORTS: THE LATE 1980s

The final push to influence United States acid rain policy making came primarily from the Canadian Coalition on Acid Rain (CCAR). This organization was the focal point of Canadian lobbying in the United States. Although it was partially supported by government funds, the CCAR did not ask for, or receive, official status as a representative of the Canadian government. In fact, this organization frequently found itself acting contrary to the wishes of the Canadian government. It spent some of its time railing against Canadian inadequacies. Simply put, its overall goal was to reduce acid rain pollutants by 50 percent, in *both* the United States and Canada. This meant that if at times members of the CCAR had to criticize their own government's policies, they would do so.

At the beginning of the acid rain debate in the early 1980s, the CCAR was openly provocative. By the middle 1980s, however, this stance had altered. The CCAR had quietly retreated from the public view and began a behind-the-scenes campaign dedicated to the careful and deliberate control of information. Adele Hurley, codirector of the Coalition, outlined the goals of the CCAR in her testimony before the United States Congress: "[T]his coalition will work with a variety of American interest groups to develop and maintain channels to the memberships of those groups. We will seek to distribute information to their members through their newsletters and magazines. We will call on the grassroots for support through mass mailing and newspaper appeals. We will seek meetings with the press and media to reach out beyond the membership groups" (U.S. Congress. Senate. Committee on Environment and Public Works 1981, 45).

While it took some time for these efforts to coalesce, by the late 1980s the CCAR was in full operation. It is important to note that this effort by the Canadians differed sharply from the high rhetoric of the initial Canadian public relations campaign. There was a clear shift in strategy as well as a distinct attempt to blend into the United States political landscape; to behave like any other United States interest group lobbying for change.

And, while not working together in any formal capacity, the official Canadian government lobby also changed its focus to behind-the-scenes grassroots lobbying.[7] It was not that this type of effort had not been made before this time, but by the middle-to-late 1980s, it became the primary way in which the Canadian government carried out its campaign to shift United States policy concerning acid rain. While Prime Minister Mulroney continued to advocate for Canada at the presidential level, the CCAR and representatives of the Canadian Embassy were very hard at work at the grassroots level of United States politics. The Canadians took great advantage of one source of input: their links to the members of Congress who were friendly to their position. Most of these links were with people from border states, especially those in the Northeast (the region of the United States most adversely affected by acid rain). Yet, these links were not limited to this particular geographic area, just as they were not limited to a particular political affiliation. The only real limiting factors were sympathy and concern for the Canadian perspective.

The Canadians worked hard on these linkages, especially those with congressional staff members. As a member of the CCAR explained to me:

> We targeted certain states and groups. We knew we would never get Ohio so we just wrote them off. We concentrated on what we believed were crucial, swing delegations, like Pennsylvania. Staff members would call and say "congressman so-and-so is proposing this" and we'd say whether it was good or bad. Sometimes we would even write it up for them. But nobody knew it was us. You just couldn't say it was the Coalition. We were information brokers. We provided information at strategic times. We worked with Americans who believed what we did. We were their retrievers. Any time they needed information, we got it for them.[8]

At great disadvantage within the United States political system because they did not represent a United States constituency, the Canadians focused on the best tool they had available: information, especially scientific information. They became brokers in information and were especially adept at using scientific studies completed in the United States. Seldom did they argue from the basis of Canadian scientific studies, although these were readily available and credible. Rather, they fed members of Congress, the public, environmental groups, and anyone who would listen with data and information from the United States scientific community. Studies from the General Accounting Office, Congressional Research Service, Environmental Protection Agency, and National Academy of Sciences were promoted, as well as other scientific research conducted by United States scientists at United States universities. The idea was to convince the people of the United States that acid rain was a serious problem, not just because of its adverse effects in Canada, but because of the adverse effects it was causing in the United States. In other words, the goal had become to convince United States policy makers that they had a serious *domestic* acid rain problem. And what better way to do that than to provide evidence from members of their own (United States) scientific community?

The grass-roots effort by the CCAR is estimated to have cost $3.6 million over 10 years and involved all the activities associated with United States lobbyists (Spears 1990, C6). Members of the CCAR spoke at local meetings, fed information to low-level political aides, circulated at countless cocktail parties, and developed a high-level information base (Gorrie 1990, C1). But this effort was different in a number of ways from those of typical United States lobbyists. The Canadians' primary focus was to help other lobbying groups, especially United States environmental groups that were pushing an agenda favorable to Canadian desires. In this effort, the Canadians were essentially in a supporting role, a role that kept them behind the scenes and unobtrusive. It was very important to the Canadians to be viewed as helping the process, rather than demanding action.

However, it must always be remembered that Canada and its representatives are more than just another lobbying group. Canada is the United States' biggest trading partner, closest ally, and—above all—a foreign country. Its leader has direct access to the President and hence, instant legitimacy on international issues. Still, this is not necessarily a plus when lobbying in the United States, and the Canadians were well aware of this. The Canadians made a genuine effort to always remain aware that they were foreigners in the United States. That is why they placed an emphasis on using United States scientific data as the basis for their arguments, why they established a position in a supporting role, and why the shift to a behind-the-scenes effort was made. The Canadians did not want a repeat of the intensive negative reaction they received in their initial frontal assault on the United States political system.

The answer to the question of whether the Canadians were successful in their bid to influence the United States acid rain policy must be speculative, primarily because the push for a United States policy was not solely a Canadian endeavor. Many individuals and groups within the United States had been promoting change for a long time. To filter out only Canadian influences would be impossible. Nevertheless, there are indications that the Canadians did, indeed, play a role in the formulation of this particular domestic environmental policy.

First, some scholars who have studied the United States–Canadian acid rain debate credit Canada with influencing United States decision making. While Don Munton asserted that it would be easy to exaggerate the influence Canada had on the acid rain debate, he also stated that Canada, undoubtedly, did have some influence (Munton 1997b, 19). Everett Cataldo pointed out that when the acid rain debate was finally settled, the Bush administration acknowledged Canada as a legitimate player in the politics of acid rain policy formation (1992, 406). Further, Cataldo suggested that "Canada's policy demands figured seriously in the administration's selection of policy options. . . . Canada's unflagging advocacy of a bilateral solution to the acid rain problem put considerable pressure on the Bush administration to address Canada's concerns as well as U.S. domestic interests in its formulation of policy to deal with the [acid rain] problem" (1992, 407).

Second, interviews of congressional staff members whose expertise lay in the environmental arena suggest that Canadian lobbying on the acid rain issue during the 1980s may have been effective in some instances.[9] A good number of congressional staff members viewed the Canadian lobbying effort as a blatant interference in United States domestic policy making. A range of attitudes was represented by these staff members, from those who said that Canada should clean up its own back yard before trying to make the United States accountable to those who pointed to the Canadian secret agenda of selling more electrical power to the United States. One staff member from a midwestern state summed up this point of view by offering the author the following observations: "Canada is a sovereign country and should not interfere in our domestic policy. Sure, I believe that they have been successful, but their lobbying turns me off. I don't go up there and lobby them when they are debating legislation. They have the habit of telling us what to do when in fact their national program is unenforceable." This group generally believed that Canadian lobbying really hurt the overall Canadian effort because of the ill feelings it created. They felt that the Canadian lobbying actually detracted from Canada's ultimate goal.

A second group of staff members felt that the Canadian effort was so regional in nature that it did not have much of an effect. Several mountain-state staff members remarked that the Canadian lobby was not effective because it focused only on the Northeast. One went so far as to argue that the Canadian effort in the Northeast was all right, because the West was not affected by acid rain, anyway. On the other hand, one staff member declared that "since we're from Ohio, Canada just does not play a role in formulating our views." The general attitude of respondents in this group was that Canada played only a marginal role outside of the Northeast border-states.

A third group, however, felt that the Canadians had had a substantial and lasting effect. This group was dominated by staff members who had regular contact with the Canadians. One staff member was impressed that the Canadians called him on the very day that President Bush announced his acid rain proposal. Another said that her visit (which was paid for by the Canadians) to the affected area in Canada had an overwhelming impact on how she viewed United States policy and that it was hard to overstate the importance of Canada's efforts. A border state staff member remarked that "the Canadians are our allies and I work with them all the time." He went on to observe that this relationship had worked for him but that he had to be very careful about what he said and had to keep a low profile in terms of his involvement with the Canadians. This particular staff member confided that he worried about saying something that could be misconstrued in any way to reflect a Canadian slant on the acid rain issue.

This final group was also impressed with the amount and accuracy of the information provided by Canada. They said that the Canadians always put forward well-documented scientific results and talked about the significance of the accumulating scientific evidence. There was a general belief that the Canadians were sensitive about criticizing the United States and that they were making a conscious effort to work at the lower levels of government, to lay the groundwork for their views and find common ground anywhere they could.

AN OVERVIEW OF CANADIAN EFFORTS

Throughout the 1980s, Canadians used a multifaceted foreign policy approach in hopes of gaining their single most important environmental policy objective— the reduction of transboundary flows of acid pollutants. At one time or another, Canadians attempted to influence United States acid rain policy decisions through quiet diplomacy (formal diplomatic avenues), interventionist public diplomacy (going public), international diplomacy (agreements and conferences), personal diplomacy (interactions between the Prime Minister and the President), and strengthening their own domestic environmental programs (Munton and Castle 1992, 322–27).

Moreover, Canadians went far beyond their normal diplomatic activities and directly intervened in the United States political process. Disregarding a long tradition of noninterference in United States domestic policy making, Canadians (at both the national and provincial levels) extended their efforts to include directly lobbying the United States public, media, nongovernmental organizations, and Congress. In essence, Canadians resorted to a lobbying effort clearly in line with any other United States lobby. This effort was not only substantial (millions of dollars were spent), it was also clearly not consistent with what Canadians had previously perceived as normal behavior in the Canada–United States bilateral relationship.

To understand how and why the Canadians chose to behave in the role of a traditional United States interest group, one must first understand that all Canada–United States environmental relations with respect to acid rain are based upon dependency and asymmetry. As John Carroll (1982, 1986), Stephen Clarkson (1983), and Don Munton (1981) have so often pointed out, factors such as the total emissions of pollutants, meteorology, the prevailing weather, geology, and the varying capacity of the terrain to neutralize damage have established a multidimensional problem whereby the United States benefits much less from Canadian actions than Canada does from United States actions.

Because of this imbalance, the Canadians well understood that their hopes of reducing cross-border air pollution rested with the United States' will (and ability) to develop a domestic policy to reduce the precursors of acid rain. In this regard, Canadians took full advantage of a United States political system that allows groups to mobilize and countermobilize in their efforts to create monopolies on political understandings of policy issues (Baumgartner and B. Jones 1993, 1–24). The Canadians also understood that those interests that possess issue-specific knowledge (e.g., scientific knowledge) are not only in a position to respond quickly and with greater accuracy than those without such information, they are also better equipped to identify the value implications of this knowledge and employ it to influence government elites in the direction of their policy preferences (Steger et al. 1987, 1–4).

The Canadians made a carefully organized effort to develop a policy niche in the United States domestic political arena. There was a conscious effort to use scientific information as a way to influence members of the United States Congress. The Canadians were quite successful in establishing themselves as an efficient and credible source of scientific information on the acid rain issue. At any time that policy makers, interest groups, the media, or simply a member of the public wanted scientific information related to acid rain, they could get a quick and comprehensive reply from the Canadians. As a high ranking Canadian lobbyist told me:

We had to make a base and establish a reputation. And it had to be credible and consistent. We had to let everyone know we were in it for the long term and that they could call our number at any time and we would be there. We put down roots. In Washington, D.C. information is your currency and we had to be right because that's all we had. No one had any ties to us.

All things considered, Canadians saw the United States government eventually recognize acid rain as a serious environmental problem and agree to substantially reduce the production of transboundary pollutants. However, for a long period of time, those that opposed additional controls to reduce acid rain were successful at redirecting the acid rain issue away from what the Canadians were promoting; the environmental dangers of acid rain. The leadership of the United States coal and utility industries helped redefine acid rain as a fairness issue by bringing attention to the fact that Canada's environmental laws were inferior to those of the United States. They were also able to introduce doubt about Canadian claims of concern over acid rain. They accomplished this by drawing attention to the certainty that Canada would benefit economically by selling excess electrical power to the United States if coal-fired utilities in the United States had to reduce their pollution levels. Further, John Dingell (and others) succeeded at turning the discussion about acid rain pollution into a discussion about how the Canadians were really interfering in what should be a purely United States domestic policy debate.

Clearly, these efforts by those opposed to acid rain controls reframed the acid rain debate. Canadians withdrew from their frontal attacks on the United States. They then refocused their efforts on a behind-the-scene drive to use scientific information to quietly lobby interest groups and members of Congress whom they believed were supportive of their views. In the end, both the Canadian government and nongovernment entities' efforts to provide scientific information to United States individuals and groups deserve at least partial credit for bringing about United States action to reduce acid rain pollution.

NOTES

1. For a more comprehensive look at the Canadian connection to United States acid rain policy making, see Carroll (1986), Munton (1997a, 1997b) and Schmandt, Clarkson, and Roderick (1988).

2. Kal Holsti summed up what had generally been perceived as the normal view of United States–Canadian relations up to this time: "[C]onflicts of interest and diplomatic irritations are essentially 'problems' to be solved rather than major confrontations to be won at all costs through campaigns and stratagems of diplomacy and threats" (1971, 383).

3. John Kirton has described Canada as the "first and most active participant in penetrating the thin wall of sovereignty between the two countries, with extensive efforts at public diplomacy, and lobbying Congress and American interest groups, on a host of trade issues and, most certainly, acid rain " (1993, 296–97).

4. The issue of Canadian lobbying and interference with United States domestic policy making was certainly brought into focus when the United States Justice Department decided to classify these two films on acid rain (produced by the National Film Board of Canada) as political propaganda (Davis 1983a, 1065).

5. Just because the Canadians were not physically present at the initial hearings did not mean they were forgotten. At the very first hearing on acid rain in the House of Representatives, Representative Jerome Ambro of New York cited the bitter complaining of the Canadians as a motivation to act (U.S. Congress. House of Representatives. Committee on Science and Technology, Subcommittee on Natural Resources, Agricultural Research and Environment 1980, 145). In the Senate, that same spring,

Senator Percy of Illinois stated that he was "fully sensitive to the warnings of the Canadian officials" (U.S. Congress. House of Representatives. Committee on Energy and Natural Resources, Subcommittee on Energy Regulation 1980, 84) and EPA administrator Douglas Costle noted, "The Canadians are most concerned about acid rain and what we are doing about it, especially since they import from us about three times the amount of acid rain–causing pollutants than they export to us" (U.S. Congress. Senate. Committee on Energy and Natural Resources, Subcommittee on Energy Regulation 1980, 165).

6. In the end, Canadian federal and provincial environment ministers met and agreed that they would develop a Canadian reduction program that would not be contingent on United States action. They also revised upward their estimates of the 1980 emissions that provided the benchmark for the 50 percent reduction figure (Macdonald 1997, 9).

7. In fact, Allan Gotlieb (Canadian Ambassador to Washington, D.C., from 1981 to 1989) stated that "In Washington . . . the Canadian Embassy might be readily compared with a domestic lobby group which cultivates, issue by issue, key players in the executive branch, the media, and especially Capital Hill" (Jockel 1990, 6).

8. These comments, as well as all the other comments presented in this chapter in this manner, are gleaned from interviews conducted by the author as explained in Chapter 1.

9. These interviews were part of the overall collection of data as described in Chapter 1. In this particular instance, the results are based on interviews of 41 congressional staff members who were directly involved in the development of United States acid rain legislation. Most of those interviewed worked for members of the Senate who served on the Environment and Public Works Committee ·or the Environment Protection Subcommittee (n=22), or worked for members of the House who served on the Energy and Commerce Committee or the Health and Environment Subcommittee (n=19).

Chapter 4

Science, Scientists, and Acid Rain

INTRODUCTION

It is generally accepted that scientists are a major source of knowledge and expertise in dealing with many of the complex issues (e.g., health care and environmental degradation) that affect our everyday lives. Scientists are viewed as directly influencing the policy-making process by determining alternatives, proposals, and solutions to public policy problems (Kingdon 1995, 68–70). In this regard, scientists are considered of central importance to the environmental policy-making process, because they provide policy makers with information and expertise gained through the gradual accumulation of knowledge and through scientific discovery. Among other activities, scientists give testimony before Congress, write professional papers, prepare speeches, provide information to the press, and criticize one another's work. By these efforts, scientists are supposed to help decision-makers solve whatever serious problems are facing the nation. But was this true for the issue of acid rain pollution?

We have seen (from the previous chapters) that acid rain was a highly contentious issue on which policy makers received advice from a multitude of sources. By the time the acid rain debate began in earnest in the United States (in the early 1980s), there existed an abundance of peer-reviewed scientific studies that carefully delineated the nature of acid rain.[1]

Scientists had been conducting research on acid rain for some time, although scientific recognition of this particular transborder pollution (despite President Carter's initial recognition) was not immediately translated into an important domestic, bilateral, or international policy issue. This chapter highlights the role that scientists played in the development of a United States policy to reduce acid rain pollution and shows that, in many instances, scientific input was highly controversial and sometimes of limited value.

This chapter epitomizes Kingdon's suggestion that the key to understanding the policy process is being able to explain how particular problems get joined to particular solutions. Scientists are continually asked to join solutions to problems and to make those connections in a way that is not only supported by rigorous research, but is also politically feasible. The following sections delineate how difficult the joining of problems to solutions can be. There is a discussion of how scientists defined the acid rain issue in a way that redirected attention away from the costs of acting toward the costs of not acting. In addition, the interaction between scientists and policy makers is described in a way that highlights the contrast between the different view each of these professions has of the world and shows how these differences can delay, and even prevent, the policy streams from converging.

THE BEGINNING OF THE ACID RAIN DEBATE

In the case of acid rain, scientists played a unique and active role in bringing the issue to the United States public's and government's attention. Many scientists actively sought publicity for their concerns about acid rain and used not only the presentation of papers and lectures to their learned colleagues but the media as well to dramatize the possibly catastrophic consequences of the continued presence of acid rain.

Although it was in the 1870s that the Englishman Robert Smith coined the term "acid rain" and provided the first comprehensive analysis of acid rain's effects,[2] it was the Canadian Eville Gorham (a professor of ecology at the University of Minnesota) who laid the North American foundation for our present understanding of the causes and impacts of acid rain (Cowling 1982, 111–12A). Through a long series of papers published in the late 1950s and early 1960s, Gorham documented the effects of acid precipitation. He concluded that acid precipitation was not only related to the deterioration of soils and lakes but was related to the incidence of bronchitis in humans.

At first, Gorham's work went largely unnoticed by the scientific community as well as by the public at large. It has been suggested that this was probably due to the fact that Gorham's work was highly interdisciplinary and published in a diverse array of scientific journals (Cowling 1982, 112A). But Gorham's work gained much more attention when, in 1967 and 1968, Swedish scientist Svante Odén published a series of newspaper accounts about the possibility of acid rain leading to a chemical war among the nations of Europe. At the time, Odén's ideas that acid rain was a large-scale regional phenomenon and that pollutants could travel long distances (up to 22 kilometers) were considered both unconventional and highly controversial. Further, the use of the term "war" to describe a situation that involved the long-range transport of chemical pollutants was considered downright outrageous and sparked genuine excitement among the public and the scientific community. As noted by one prominent United States scientist, "[Odén's] conclusions and hypotheses led to a veritable storm of scientific and public concern about acid precipitation. Suddenly, limnological, agricultural, and atmospheric scientists began to argue and debate with each other about Odén's unconventional ideas and his general theory of atmospheric influences" (Cowling 1982, 115A).

The controversy and excitement that captured so much European attention followed Odén to North America in the early 1970s, where he presented a series of lectures at various institutes in the United States and Canada. Odén's presence and his continued insistence that dangerous chemicals could be transported hundreds of miles via the atmosphere proved to be the needed stimulus for significant scientific interest in acid rain in North America (Gould 1985, 17). Shortly after Odén's lecture series, serious scientific work involving acid rain began in earnest and, by the mid-1970s, numerous publications about acid rain were appearing in both technical journals and in popular magazines like *Scientific American* (Kahan 1986, 6–7). Furthermore, comprehensive research projects were started at major universities in Canada and the United States, with such noted scientists as Richard Beamish, Harold Harvey, Eville Gorham of Canada as well as Gene Likens,[3] Charles Cogbill, Carl Schofield, and James Galloway of the United States producing a series of publications on acid rain pollution in North America (Cowling 1982, 117A; Israelson 1990, 165–72).

The work of these and other researchers in documenting acid rain as one of the most important environmental problems to face North America played a major role in transforming acid rain from "an esoteric topic of scientific research in certain specialized fields of ecology and atmospheric chemistry into a household word" (Regens and Rycroft 1988, 3). In fact, much of the credit for successful legislation and the signing of the Air Quality Accord went to scientists, who played a substantial part in defining acid rain as a serious North American environmental concern.

DEFINING ACID RAIN

Scientists were responsible for defining the acid rain issue and setting the context in which the debate would be held. According to one group of researchers, the acid rain issue came into prominence because a small community of acid rain scientists kept telling other scientists (through the presentation of papers and lectures at professional and scholarly gatherings) of its potential devastating effects (Schmandt, Clarkson, and Roderick 1988, 118). Many of the scientists doing research on acid rain went beyond simply turning their research findings over to policy makers and going about their work as usual. Instead, they actively attempted to publicize their concerns about acid rain, using the mass media as a forum for discussion of what they viewed as a serious environmental problem.

To this end, many scientists found themselves helping to establish the importance of acid rain as a policy issue. According to the Office of Technology Assessment, the acid rain policy debate centered around the problems of balancing concerns for economic well-being with concerns for natural and human resources as well as whether additional scientific research was likely "to provide significant, near-term policy guidance, or resolve value conflicts" (U.S. Office of Technology Assessment 1984, 3). Essentially, the question for policy makers became whether to act immediately or wait for further scientific information. Delaying action might risk further ecological damage, while acting immediately could waste millions of dollars on a deficient abatement program. The key to answering this policy question lay in dealing with questions about the seriousness of the acid rain problem, the causes and effects of acid rain, the effectiveness of the proposed solutions, and who was to blame for acid rain (Gould 1985; Kahan 1986; Regens and Rycroft 1988).

Attempting to answer these questions resulted in an often contentious and bitter policy debate. Richard Barton spoke of the acid rain debate during this period of time as taking on "a sinister confrontational tone that continued to escalate" (1990, 70) and John Carroll observed that the acid rain debate "during some of its less diplomatic moments might well have given the uninitiated an impression that economic sanctions—if not war outright—would soon become inevitable" (1991, 15).

During the debate over the issue of acid rain, the scientific community did not speak with one voice. As Robert Lackey and Roger Blair pointed out, because advocates from opposing sides (those for and those against acid rain controls) used scientific research to support their own positions or to disparage those of their opponents, scientists tended to get classified as being from one side or the other (1997, 9). There was also tension between United States and Canadian scientists. At one point during the debate, Canadian scientists accused United States scientists of manipulating facts and figures to achieve desired results and deliberately releasing ambiguous information to the public (Glode and Glode 1993, 28). In short, the scientific dialogue about acid rain was characterized by "disagreements, accusations, and rancorous language" (Rhodes and Middleton 1983b, 34).

POLITICS AND SCIENCE

In the early days of the United States policy debate over acid rain, Anne LaBastille submitted that "The dilemma of acid rain will ultimately be solved by politicians, economists and the public, acting on the best information we scientists bring forth" (1981, 676). As the debate moved well into the 1980s, some scientists continued to believe that LaBastille was correct. I. J. Wilk claimed that because scientists were the only ones with the proper background to evaluate claims and counterclaims about acid rain, it was their responsibility to come forward as an impartial source of information (1985, 294). Along this same line of thought, Janet Johnson proclaimed that it was scientific knowledge that laid the foundation for the policy response of the United States to the problem of acid rain (1985, 271).

Yet, others were much more skeptical about what science and scientists could provide. William Pierson and T.Y. Chang claimed that because the biological consequences of acid rain were not well established, science could provide only circumstantial evidence of damage (1986, 167). Don Munton referred to the lack of "a broad scientific consensus" (1983, 15), and James Regens pointed to the "major scientific uncertainty" surrounding the acid rain issue (1984, 310), asserting that the body of scientific information available "does not lead unequivocally to a conclusion [about] the effectiveness of proposed emissions reduction strategies" (1985, 60).

As it turned out, the fact that scientists could not provide an unequivocal answer (solution) to the acid rain problem became a major focus of the acid rain policy debate among policy makers. A glance at some of the testimony given by scientists at congressional hearings on acid rain provides insight into the difficulty of being able to mesh science with policy.

Scientific Testimony

The list of scientists who provided testimony about the acid rain issue at congressional hearings reads like a "who's who" of acid rain researchers: Svante Odén, Eville Gorham, Ellis Cowling, Gene Likens, James Galloway, and on and on. Yet, right from the start of scientists' testimonies and discussions with lawmakers, it was clear that scientists and policy makers had different expectations about what scientists should provide.

In one of the very first hearings in the United States Senate, Ellis Cowling (Professor of Plant Pathology and Forest Resources at North Carolina State University) and Senator Paul Tsongas of Massachusetts attempted to set the tone for scientific testimony on acid rain. Cowling saw his role and the role of policy makers as follows: "I am, of course, a scientist and not a politician. And it is my duty to provide you with the scientific assessment of the facts, and I guess it is the duty of the politician to make decisions" (U.S. Congress. Senate. Committee on Energy and Natural Resources 1980, 7). Tsongas' remarks suggested that he understood the dichotomy between scientists and policy makers as stated by Cowling, but also bemoaned the fact that decision-makers must operate under uncertainty:

The danger is that we are now in the process of making decisions, and this committee will do it tomorrow. . . . Whether or not we have adequate information is irrelevant to the decision making that is on going. The value of people like yourselves is to give us some guidance. You may be wrong but, in the land of the blind, the one eye is King. In this particular situation, I would rather have advice, even if down the road it turns out not to be correct, than no advice because that is worst of all worlds. (U.S. Congress. Senate. Committee on Energy and Natural Resources 1980, 93)

In essence, Tsongas was asking for scientists to go beyond providing only scientific information to the members of Congress. He wanted scientists to provide advice based on their special expertise. But scientists had a difficult time determining exactly what policy makers wanted and what they should actually provide, especially when it came to differentiating between fact and personal opinion.

Two exchanges between scientists and policy makers early in the acid rain debate characterize the tremendous pressure that scientists were under to provide "just the facts" without interjecting personal value judgments. The first exchange occurred when Volker Mohnen (Director of the Atmospheric Science Research Center at the State University of New York at Albany) and Gene Likens (Professor of Ecology at Cornell University) testified before the House Committee on Science and Technology in 1981. Both offered assessments of what scientists should not do. Mohnen stated:

I would not dare to confront my peers with an opinion, because we have been wrong before, sir, many times, and I think it is of no help to Congress if scientists volunteer opinions, "on the one hand," and "on the other hand." (U.S. Congress. House of Representatives. Committee on Science and Technology, Subcommittee on Natural Resources, Agricultural Research and Environment 1981, 252–53)

Likens stated:

I think one of the problems is that we have entered a realm in which we are giving our own opinions as scientists rather than our scientific evidence. (U.S. Congress. House of Representatives. Committee on Science and Technology, Subcommittee on Natural Resources, Agricultural Research and Environment 1981, 485)

The response by members of Congress to the objections of these scientists presenting their personal opinions was swift and to the point. Congressman James Scheur of New York replied:

Let me say that we want your opinions and we want your value judgments. We're going to have to make opinions and value judgments, and we really don't have the knowledge base, most of us, to do it. And since the precise knowledge base may not be existent [sic] now to make precise judgments, we have to do the best we can in this most imperfect world. And so we want your value judgments. (U.S. Congress. House of Representatives. Committee on Science and Technology, Subcommittee on Natural Resources, Agricultural Research and Environment 1981, 486)

In actuality, Scheuer is asking for scientists to act like lobbyists. He does not view the scientific community as a separate entity with a commitment to objectivity. Scheuer is working in a political world and wants advice given in political terms regardless of the consequences for the scientist and his or her standing within the scientific community.

As this exchange continued, Congresswoman Claudine Schneider of Rhode Island offered this hope:

[that] the scientific community can come to some sort of agreement on recommendations, and if not total agreement, at least general directions. . . . What I recommend to all of you, as scientists, is that you figure out what conditions you will be comfortable with and build enough of an influential body to persuade the other Members of this House who don't have the benefit or are not interested in the scientific facts, to make the right decisions for all the people. (U.S. Congress. House of Representatives. Committee on Science and Technology, Subcommittee on Natural Resources, Agricultural Research and Environment 1981, 489)

However, Congressman James Sensenbrenner of Wisconsin offered a somewhat different grasp of the situation.

I think what we are looking for, from the scientific community, is some kind of a clear answer that we can present to our colleagues. . . . The scientific community is just like a bunch of Congressmen getting together: Nobody can agree on anything and where to go. (U.S. Congress. House of Representatives. Committee on Science and Technology, Subcommittee on Natural Resources, Agricultural Research and Environment 1981, 496)

Once again, it appeared that a member of Congress failed to differentiate between scientists and other interested parties. It seems Sensenbrenner wanted scientists to provide him with some type of political cover for his views.

As he once again attempted to emphasize the basic differences between scientists and policy makers, Volker Mohnen offered the final words in this particular exchange of views:

You referred to us scientists here, that we, like you, are not fully aware of all the facts. There is one basic difference, however. If we scientists make a mistake, our peers will laugh, and that's it. To paraphrase Will Rogers, if Congress makes a mistake, it becomes law. (U.S. Congress. House of Representatives. Committee on Science and Technology, Subcommittee on Natural Resources, Agricultural Research and Environment 1981, 498)

The second exchange (documented below) illustrates the difficulty scientists seem to have when they are associated with interests that have publicly expressed their policy choices. In this case, it was Michael Oppenheimer, senior scientist at the Environmental Defense Fund (EDF) who suffered the consequences of EDF's public stand for action to reduce acid rain pollutants. He testified before the House Committee on Energy and Commerce as a spokesman for the National Clean Air Coalition (which also supported acid rain controls). Oppenheimer made it very clear where he stood.

My conclusion, as a scientist, is that enough evidence is known about the sources of acid rain to initiate a long-term control program aimed at the abatement of emissions of sulfur dioxide and oxides of nitrogen. (U.S. Congress. House of Representatives. Committee on Energy and Commerce, Subcommittee on Health and the Environment 1981a, 442)

However, Oppenheimer's assertion that he was testifying "as a scientist" came under severe criticism from Congressmen Don Ritter of Pennsylvania and Cleve Benedict of West Virginia. Oppenheimer was accused of politicizing the science and being associated with a proenvironmental group (EDF) that was perceived to be both anti-nuclear and anti-coal (U.S. Congress. House of Representatives. Committee on Energy and Commerce, Subcommittee on Health and the Environment 1981a, 470–73). Oppenheimer became so frustrated with the questioning of his scientific credentials that at one point he refused to answer a question and exclaimed "I was invited to testify here as a scientist, and not on a political issue" (U.S. Congress. House of Representatives. Committee on Energy and Commerce, Subcommittee on Health and the Environment 1981a, 466–67).

Throughout the acid rain debate, these types of exchanges about the proper role of scientific testimony were regular occurrences at congressional hearings. One person who attempted to define the line between science and politics during these exchanges between scientists and policy makers was Christopher Bernabo, executive director of the United States Interagency Task Force on Acid Precipitation. In 1981, Bernabo testified that determining how much information on acid rain was enough to make a policy decision involved value judgments and, hence, was not a scientific issue (U.S. Congress. House of Representatives. Committee on Science and Technology, Subcommittee on Natural Resources, Agricultural Research and Environment 1981, 167). In 1983, Bernabo urged members of Congress to understand that their demands for answers far exceeded what scientists could possibly provide at that time (U.S. Congress. House of Representatives. Committee on Science and Technology, Subcommittee on Natural Resources, Agricultural Research and Environment 1983, 6), and in 1985, in testimony before the House Committee on Science and Technology, he declared:

I think there is a frustration and there will continue to be a frustration in the dialogue between policy makers and scientists because in general in our society there is not a clear understanding of what their relative roles are. (U.S. Congress. House of Representatives. Committee on Science and Technology, Subcommittee on Natural Resources, Agricultural Research and Environment 1985, 41)

Many scientists expressed this frustration in testimony before Congress. James Galloway (Professor of Environmental Sciences at the University of Virginia) stated:

I have been an environmental scientist since 1968 and have been involved in studying the acid deposition issue since 1974. . . . Now, when a policy maker asks me that question, they like to have absolute answers like yes and no. As a scientist, I can't give absolute answers. (U.S. Congress. Senate. Committee on Environment and Public Works 1986, 446)

Volker Mohnen, clearly frustrated by the constant questioning about the uncertainty of the scientific method, challenged lawmakers in a way that left no doubt about how he felt:

If you fault the Academy [the National Academy of Sciences], if you fault any scientist for learning on a day-to-day basis, and having and being able to accept the new knowledge, if you condemn this, then you should never call scientists on the witness bench. (U.S. Congress. House of Representatives. Committee on Energy and Commerce, Subcommittee on Health and the Environment 1984b, 972)

During the acid rain debate carried out in the United States Congress, scientists were continually asked to make value judgments about their research and give personal opinions about what should be done. However, many scientists (as quoted above) were quite uncomfortable with this effort by policy makers and responded accordingly. Nonetheless, the questions kept coming and —as will be seen—many scientists remain frustrated at the inability of policy makers to distinguish between what scientists believe are significant differences between scientific findings and value judgments.

The Linearity Issue

Two of the most contentious scientific controversies that pervaded the debate about acid rain were:

(1) The linearity versus nonlinearity issue; that is, whether further reduction in sulfur dioxide (SO_2) and nitrogen oxides (NO_x) would produce equivalent reductions in sulfate and nitrate deposition, and

(2) The local versus long-range sources issue; that is, whether "local" emissions of SO_2 and NO_x influence acid deposition levels in sensitive areas as much, or more than, "long-range" transportation of these precursors of acid rain. (Freeman 1985, 286–97)

Instead of scientific consensus on these two areas of concern, an emotional scientific debate took place that was publicly aired.

In 1983, the National Academy of Sciences (NAS) released a report titled *Acid Deposition: Atmospheric Processes in Eastern North America.* Some researchers thought that this NAS report had put to rest the linearity question once and for all, and stated:

According to a report published in 1983, we can now conclude unequivocally that in eastern North America average annual emission of sulfur dioxide from power plants and other industrial facilities is roughly proportional to deposition of sulfate. (Schmandt, Clarkson, and Roderick 1988, 8)

However, the unquestionable faith in the conclusion of this NAS report was not shared by all. Larry Parker and John Blodgett argued that the 1977 Amendments to the Clean Air Act were inadequate in dealing with acid deposition because they addressed only the emitted pollutants (SO_2 and NO_x) and not the different chemical forms of sulfates and nitrates that actually make up acid rain (1985, 110). Glenn Gibian (after reviewing the reliabilities of several long-range transport models) asserted, "Even such drastic measures as total elimination of sulfur dioxide emissions from all power plants is predicted to result in a small decrease in rainfall activity—even by the most 'optimistic' model" (1985, 164).

It is obvious from the reactions noted above that the 1983 NAS report did not provide either comprehensive or definitive answers to the linearity puzzle. In fact, if one goes by the furor created at congressional hearings and in the media shortly following the release of this report, one could easily draw the conclusion that it created more confusion than consensus.

Archie Kahan (1986) detailed what happened when two prominent and well-respected scientists (Jack Calvert and Bernard Manowitz) publicly clashed over the results of the 1983 NAS report. Jack Calvert was the senior scientist at the National Center for Atmospheric Research and chaired the National Academy of Sciences National Research Council, which published the NAS report that concluded that there was an approximate one-to-one linearity between emissions of sulfur dioxide and acid rainfall. Despite the fact that this conclusion was corroborated by a group of scientists assembled under the direction of the White House Office of Science and Technology Policy, the chairman of the Science and Technology Committee of the House of Representatives (Don Fuqua) questioned the results. Fuqua requested an independent evaluation of the NAS report by the Department of Energy. To complete the evaluation, the National Laboratory Consortium was formed under the leadership of Bernard Manowitz, a senior scientist from the Brookhaven National Laboratory.

This consortium consisted of scientists from Brookhaven, Argonne National Laboratory, Oak Ridge National Laboratory, and Battelle Northwest Laboratory. Manowitz's scientific research group, after careful analysis, not only disagreed with the methods that the Calvert group had used to produce its findings, but—using the same data—came to just the opposite conclusion: that a nonlinear relationship existed. What really fueled the debate was the wide circulation the Manowitz report received. Apparently, Manowitz distributed his report to the leadership and research arms of the power industry and related industries as well as to the administrative and legislative staffs of both the federal and state governments. The results were introduced into the Congressional Record and were adopted by the electric utility industry as being clear evidence that reducing SO_2 and NO_x would not solve the acid rain problem.

Jack Calvert's testimony before Congress in September 1983 depicts his frustration and concerns about the attack on his (and the National Research

Council's) work. Calvert first expressed his reluctance to publicly discuss what he believed to be an internal scientific debate and asked the members of the House not to take his words as a personal attack on any single individual. Calvert further stated that even though Congress was not well suited to carry out a scientific debate, he felt compelled to "at least stand up for my committee" (U.S. Congress. House of Representatives. Committee on Science and Technology, Subcommittee on Natural Resources, Agricultural Research and Environment 1983, 52). Calvert then chastised the Manowitz report because it was released and directed, not to his peers in the scientific community, but to the political parties in the acid rain debate (e.g., the leadership of the power industry and the selected members of the administrative and legislative staffs of the federal and state governments who had been critical of Calvert's findings). In conclusion, Calvert proclaimed his disgust and embarrassment about having to carry out this scientific debate within the Halls of Congress and asserted:

Our conclusions represent the best judgment of a group of highly qualified and diversified scientists and we certainly would not alter or compromise these conclusions on the basis of any unusual review of the Manowitz group. (U.S. Congress. House of Representatives. Committee on Science and Technology, Subcommittee on Natural Resources, Agricultural Research and Environment 1983, 53)

Contrary to what Calvert wished, the debate over whose science was correct ended up being carried out in the public arena, with charges and counter-charges that each of these scientists' (Calvert and Manowitz) work was unprofessional and "seriously flawed scientifically" (Kahan 1986, 148). Thus, a scientific debate carried out on the floor of Congress and in the national media helped transform questions about the relationship between emissions of acid precursors (SO_2 and NO_x) and acid deposition into an argument over which scientific groups were correct in their analysis and who did, or did not, use improper scientific procedures.

The Local Versus Long-Range Issue

The local versus long-range issue (i.e., whether the local emissions of SO_2 and NO_x or the long-range transported pollutants cause the most significant damage) provides another example of how public scientific debate led to questions about the ability of scientists to produce a solution to the acid deposition problem. Roy Gould (1985) described how a few nationally known scientists cast doubt on what was, presumably, a scientific consensus on the source of acid rain. Several scientific reports (including the 1983 NAS report discussed above) had indicated "that in order to significantly reduce acid rain in the Adirondacks, one would have [to] reduce emissions in the Ohio Valley/Midwest" (Gould 1985, 100). However, using the *New York Times* and National Public Radio as means of communication, A. Gordon Everett (who was hired by Consolidated Edison) and Volker Mohnen (who had been retained by Peabody Coal, the nation's largest coal company) disputed the results of the NAS report and argued that "the contribution of midwestern sources to acid rain in the Northeast remains unknown" (Gould 1985, 104).

The debate took a different turn in early 1982 when Kenneth Rahn (a prominent atmospheric chemist with the Graduate School of Oceanography at the University of Rhode Island) produced a three-page document claiming that the oft-quoted attribution of the Northeast's acid rain to the long-range transport of pollution from the Midwest might be an oversimplification (Kerr 1982, 881). Rahn's informal statements caused something of an uproar in environmental circles in Washington, D.C. and became the focal point of hearings in the United States Congress. In releasing his statement, Rahn stated that while his data "cast considerable doubt on the popular view of the Midwest as the dominant source of acidity throughout the Northeast," it was also preliminary and incomplete (U.S. Congress. Senate. Committee on Environment and Public Works 1982, 22). Rahn made it very clear at the time of the release of his study that his results should be used with caution (Kerr 1982, 881). However, that did not happen.

As soon as Rahn made his preliminary results public, they were introduced into the congressional record by the Reagan administration. Kathleen Bennett, the EPA's assistant administrator for Air, Noise, and Radiation, acknowledged that Rahn's work was preliminary and not subject to peer review, but claimed that there was now scientific evidence indicating "that acid deposition in the Northeastern States may be derived from SO_2 emissions of local origin rather than from the Midwest as commonly perceived" (U.S. Congress. Senate. Committee on Foreign Relations, Subcommittee on Arms Control, Oceans, International Operations and Environment 1982, 104). Soon thereafter, Rahn was called in front of the Senate Committee on Environment and Public Works to defend his research findings.

As he did when his statement was originally released, Rahn made it very plain at the beginning of his testimony that the evidence he had was largely preliminary, incomplete, and not the result of any formal, funded study (U.S. Congress. Senate. Committee on Environment and Public Works 1982, 20). He also stated that his study was "the result of not large amounts of effort on our part. It is something which is a spin-off of another study. We have not to date had the luxury of going into the detail of examining all aspects of this problem" (U.S. Congress. Senate. Committee on Environment and Public Works 1982, 72–73).

Rahn also defended his belief that most of the acidity in the Northeast might be local in origin. He expressed his personal view that there was no ecological crisis that demanded rapid action, that it might be best to wait a few years for more research to become available and that, furthermore:

[t]o legislate strong controls on certain pollutants before the entire system is understood, especially when those controls are focused on one area of the country, seems to me to be

several years premature at best and potentially disastrous economically at worst. (U.S. Congress. Senate. Committee on Environment and Public Works 1982, 22)

After listening to Rahn testify, Senator George Mitchell of Maine attacked Rahn's credibility and called his recommendations "baffling" (U.S. Congress. Senate. Committee on Environment and Public Works 1982, 73). Senator Mitchell challenged Rahn even further:

I find it incredible that on the basis of admitted part-time, spare time study, as a spin-off of something else, in an area that you had no previous experience with, that involves 10 percent of the problem, you come in here and make a very emphatic and specific recommendation, 'Here is what we should do. Here is what we shouldn't do.' It just strikes me that the level of recommendation bears no relationship to the effort that went into the studies. (U.S. Congress. Senate. Committee on Environment and Public Works 1982, 73)

It appears that despite Rahn's insistence that his research findings were preliminary, incomplete, and to be used with caution, once both his scientific findings and his personal views were made public (as a statement released to his colleagues, as the topic of an article in *Science*, and eventually at congressional hearings), Rahn's statements were used time and again throughout the rest of the year to bolster the side that did not want acid rain controls put into place. As Kathleen Bennett put it when referring to Rahn's research findings:

The American people have the right to expect that their Government will not impose an additional multi-billion-dollar pollution control program . . . without first determining with some assurance that the intended environmental benefits will be achieved. (U.S. Congress. Senate. Committee on Foreign Relations, Subcommittee on Arms Control, Oceans, International Operations and Environment 1982, 104)

The Art of Delay

These differing views about the state of the science allowed proponents of inaction to make the case that policy decisions should not be finalized until there existed a clear and definitive scientific consensus on the causes and effects of acid rain. Industry spokesmen (especially for coal and utility industries) as well as the Reagan administration used these scientific disagreements over acid rain to call for further research and study before evoking any abatement action. As Regens and Rycroft pointed out during the debate, "the scientific information currently available does not lead unequivocally to a conclusion about whether it is appropriate to begin additional control measures now or to await better understanding" (1988, 135).

The fact that studies by the National Academy of Sciences (one of the most prestigious and most respected scientific bodies in North America) could be so effectively challenged in both the public and scientific arenas created the impression that scientists could not (at this particular time) agree that acid rain was even a problem. Hence, parties that wished to delay or inhibit action were left with a powerful justification for inaction: the common and well-used refrain, "we need more (and better) science."

No one used this refrain more consistently or effectively than President Reagan and others in his administration. For example, when the National Academy of Sciences published a 1981 report entitled *Atmospheric-Biosphere Interactions*, which not only documented the high acidity of rainfall in the Northeast but suggested that a 50 percent reduction in SO_2 emissions would be an appropriate action, President Reagan dismissed the NAS report as lacking in objectivity (Gould 1985, 91) and quickly found experts who supported his point of view (Marshall 1982, 1118–19).[4] At the same time, the Environmental Protection Agency (working under the direction of President Reagan) warned that "scientific uncertainties in the causes and effects of acid rain demand that we proceed cautiously and avoid premature action" (Gould 1985, 89).

Then, in 1983, a group of nine nationally known scientists (working under the auspices of the White House Office of Science and Technology Policy) concluded that the risks of further environmental damage outweighed the risks of acting on limited information and proposed that "[a]dditional steps should be taken now which will result in meaningful reductions in the emissions of sulfur compounds into the atmosphere" (Mosher 1983b, 1590). However, less than a month after this recommendation was made, Reagan's newly appointed director of the EPA (William Ruckelshaus) convened his own panel of 15 scientists to discuss the status of scientific knowledge with respect to acid rain. While this group of scientists agreed that reducing sulfur loadings was the most effective way to reduce acid rain pollution, it also identified a need for refinement of computer models to pinpoint the exact causes and effects of acid rain, a procedure that was estimated to take in the neighborhood of 5 additional years (Mosher 1983b, 1590–91).

Upon reflecting on these scientific findings and recommendations, President Reagan chose to ignore his own panel's recommendation for immediate action to reduce sulfur emissions and instead chose to highlight the areas of scientific uncertainty. According to some, President Reagan's response was consistent with his prior actions on the need for controlling acid rain pollution: it was one of disagreement, rejection, and a call for more studies (Wilk 1985, 295).

President Reagan also dealt a severe blow to the most significant attempt to reach a bilateral scientific consensus with Canada on acid rain. He rejected a proposal that the Royal Society of Canada and the National Academy of Sciences form a joint peer review committee to evaluate the work of the bilateral scientific groups that had been established earlier (Rhodes and Middleton 1983b, 34). Instead, President Reagan appointed a committee of reviewers under the direct control of his own science office. With this single move, the administration signaled that it wanted no part of a joint effort to reach scientific consensus on the acid rain issue. Indeed, some observers thought this action was taken so that President Reagan could keep tight control over any kind of peer-reviewed scientific work (Wilk 1985, 295–96).

In addition, President Reagan intervened in the daily operations of the United States–Canadian working groups established by the 1980 MOI. First, he replaced nearly all the senior United States university-based scientists in the working groups with junior scientists who had less experience, but were more skeptical about the dangers of acid rain (Schindler 1992, 125). Second, one of the working groups was forced to file two different reports based on the same set of scientific data—one for the Canadian side and one for the United States side—after a Reagan official joined in what many scientists viewed as a completed process. This incident is described by Orie Loucks (1993, 68–69). Apparently, after the first day of meetings in December of 1982, scientists from both the United States and Canada in Working Group 1 reported agreement on the strengths and weaknesses of the available models and on the tolerance of water sheds for acidic deposition. Then, according to Orie Loucks, a senior representative of the United States Environmental Protection Agency joined the group and told the United States scientists that they had been underestimating uncertainty in the models. The end result was that the apparent agreement reached the day before by the scientists no longer stood and two different sets of findings were written into the final report. The Canadian members of the working group concluded that about 20 percent of Ontario lakes had high acid loadings and the United States members submitted that the Canadian conclusions could not be supported by the scientific evidence.

The National Acid Precipitation Assessment Program

As referred to earlier, the National Acid Precipitation Assessment Program was authorized by Congress under the Acid Precipitation Act of 1980. Under this act, Congress directed that a comprehensive 10–year research plan be developed to complete a study of acid rain. This study was to provide information on:

- specific resources and regions affected by acidity and the extent to which acidic deposition and air pollutants contribute to those adverse effects,

- how and where emissions are transformed into acids and how they are distributed,

- whether the effects are extensive and require mitigation, and

- what emission control technologies, strategies, and mitigation options are available to reduce acidic deposition and related air pollution. (U.S. National Acid Precipitation Assessment Program 1991, 1)

NAPAP was also asked to provide annual reports to Congress on its progress. Consequently, it produced two major assessment documents: the

Interim Assessment: The Causes and Effects of Acidic Deposition, published in September of 1987; and the *1990 Integrated Assessment Report*, published in November of 1991. Both of these assessment reports came under severe criticism, albeit for different reasons. The 1987 report was swamped by charges of political interference with the science of acid rain and the 1990 report was considered quite untimely given the fact that its formal release came almost 1 year *after* Congress passed acid rain legislation. The next two sections provide a brief synopsis of the criticism that arose after the release of these NAPAP assessments and offer a glimpse into why linking science to politics can sometimes be an extremely contentious process.

The 1987 Interim Assessment Report. The release of its Interim Assessment by NAPAP in the autumn of 1987 typified the confusion surrounding the science of acid rain. At this time, many independent scientists working on acid rain research had already concluded that acid rain was a serious and urgent issue (Schmandt, Clarkson, and Roderick 1988, 255). Despite this, the executive summary of the NAPAP Interim Assessment asserted that there was little immediate danger from acid rain and that there was not much to worry about (Roberts 1987, 1404).

This finding was highly criticized, not only by the Canadians and many members of the United States Congress, but also by many of the scientists who had actually participated in the study. It was reported by Leslie Roberts that the Interim Assessment was originally scheduled for release in 1985, but the publication date was postponed several times because the report was being substantially revised by J. Laurence Kulp, the new director of research (1987, 1404). When Kulp finally released the executive summary, it was charged with being flawed, based on unrealistic projections about future emissions, and a deliberate attempt to downplay the effects of acid rain (Roberts 1987, 1404).

In addition, Kulp was accused of individually penning the executive summary in the form of a political document with no supporting data (U.S. Congress. House of Representatives. Committee on Science, Space and Technology, Subcommittee on Natural Resources, Agricultural Research and Environment 1988, 2). There were public claims by scientists that the executive summary was not only misleading and inaccurate but appeared to be directly aimed at buttressing the Reagan administration's position against controls (*Denver Post* 1987, F1). As reported by Erik Beardsley, James Gibson (who chaired the NAS Committee on long-term trends in acid deposition and contributed to the NAPAP Interim Assessment) flatly stated that the data in the three-volume report did not support the conclusions and that Kulp's interpretation of the facts "would not be supported by many of the scientists who work in the field" (1987, 7).

One of the scientists who suggested that the executive summary's conclusions did not match the scientific research was Gene E. Likens, director of the Institute of Ecosystems Studies in Millbrook, New York. Likens expressed his dismay in a letter to Congressman Gerry Sikorski (Democrat, Minnesota):

In my judgment the Executive summary for the Interim NAPAP report released last week badly misrepresented the general scientific understanding about air pollution and acid deposition. The report either ignored or discounted, out-of-hand, the thousands of articles published in high-quality scientific journals that show serious ecological damage caused by air pollution and acid deposition. . . . I urge you, while reviewing this report, to consider the enormous wealth of scientific information already published on this topic and to decouple scientific understanding from such misleading reporting. (U.S. Congress. House of Representatives. Committee on Energy and Commerce, Subcommittee on Oversight and Investigations 1987, 101)

R. Neil Sampson, executive vice president of the American Forestry Association, also expressed strong reservations about the NAPAP interim assessment executive summary, stating that the report downplayed the effects of acid deposition and that "the document [was] both slanted and potentially misleading in its presentation of the current knowledge of the effects of ozone and acid deposition on terrestrial and aquatic resources" (U.S. Congress. House of Representatives. Committee on Energy and Commerce, Subcommittee on Oversight and Investigations 1987, 125). Furthermore, Sampson voiced particular concern that scientists were being pressured not to voice their reservations about the interim assessment for fear that they would lose their federal grants if they criticized it publicly (U.S. Congress. House of Representatives. Committee on Energy and Commerce, Subcommittee on Oversight and Investigations 1987, 126).

Canadian response was just as blistering; Canada's Environment Minister described the executive summary as "incomplete and misleading" as well as "voodoo science" (U.S. Congress. House of Representatives. Committee on Energy and Commerce, Subcommittee on Oversight and Investigations 1987, 106). Several scientists also publicly castigated the report for failing to even mention Canada, where the aquatic effects were considered far more serious than in the United States (Roberts 1987, 1405). Further, one of the most well known and highly respected acid rain research scientists working in Canada (David W. Schindler) wrote a letter directly to Kulp pronouncing his disagreement with the interim report's assessment that the damage was slight. Schindler stated:

I believe that if your report is released without modification, it will only enhance the adversary positions taken between environmental groups and NAPAP, and will lead to continued erosion of respect for U.S. government science among such groups. The latter would be a particular tragedy, for I believe that the chemical, geochemical and atmospheric work done by EPA and DOE has been particularly fine, and it should not be suspected of being politicized. (U.S. Congress. House of Representatives. Committee on Energy and Commerce, Subcommittee on Oversight and Investigations 1987, 137)

Despite this firestorm of criticism, the reaction of the Reagan administration was one of complete support for the executive summary and the Director of NAPAP. EPA Administrator Thomas, in testimony before Congress, stated that the interim report and the executive summary were good documents that spoke for themselves and represented "an excellent scientific assessment of this issue" (U.S. Congress. House of Representatives. Committee on Energy and Commerce, Subcommittee on Oversight and Investigations 1987, 251).[5]

Schindler's criticism of Kulp's scientific assessment also caught the eye of John Dingell [6] (chairman of the United States House Committee on Energy and Commerce), who was one of the staunchest critics of acid rain controls and what he perceived as Canadian interference in American domestic policy making. In a string of letters to Canadian officials, members of the State Department, and acid rain scientists in both Canada and the United States, Dingell castigated Schindler for making "serious and troubling charges on Canadian stationery about alleged 'lies' on the part of Dr. Kulp" (U.S. Congress. House of Representatives. Committee on Energy and Commerce, Subcommittee on Oversight and Investigations 1987, 159) and attacked scientists in general for "advocating or supporting . . . particular [bills] or suggesting how and what legislation should be crafted to 'resolve' these problems" (U.S. Congress. House of Representatives. Committee on Energy and Commerce, Subcommittee on Oversight and Investigations 1987, 150). Dingell summarized his view as follows: "As an American, I do not take kindly to such charges against a Federal official by a non-American, particularly when that person has failed to read the entire work upon which he makes the charge. I expect and respect honest disagreements by various scientists over the research and its interpretation, but not such *in personam* attacks" (U.S. Congress. House of Representatives. Committee on energy and Commerce, Subcommittee on Oversight and Investigations (1987, 159).

In response to this criticism, Schindler wrote directly to Dingell. Among other things, Schindler pointed out that he was an American citizen, that his letter was sent before the interim report was released in an attempt to head off embarrassment of a flawed report, and that he only released copies of the letter to protect his reputation as a scientist and rapport with his colleagues. Further, Schindler stated that he was "tired of seeing the politicizing of fine research work render suspect the careers of American scientists and of seeing American environmental policy be the subject of international ridicule" (U.S. Congress. House of Representatives. Committee on Energy and Commerce, Subcommittee on Oversight and Investigations 1987, 162).

In conclusion, Schindler restated his original position, that it was obvious to the international scientific community that the severity of the acid rain problem was greatly downplayed by the NAPAP executive summary, and asked Dingell to "ensure that the final NAPAP report in 1990 accurately reflects the science of acid rain, not a distorted, politicized view" (U.S. Congress. House of Representatives. Committee on Energy and Commerce, Subcommittee on

Oversight and Investigations 1987, 164). Yet, Dingell did not appear impressed with Schindler's views and wrote back:

I can appreciate that you may disagree with various scientists, the Interim Assessment, Administration officials, and others, but I do not believe that the substance of your disagreement is enhanced by *in personam* attacks made on Canadian Government stationery that find their way to a Congressional hearing record through your scientist friends or the Canadian Ambassador. The Subcommittee is interested in learning the facts and understanding the state of the science, and is not interested in seeing its process used to express rather disparaging comments. (U.S. Congress. House of Representatives. Committee on Energy and Commerce, Subcommittee on Oversight and Investigations 1987, 200)

To be sure, the release of the NAPAP interim report and executive summary set off a series of very public disagreements involving scientists and policy makers, with all sides advocating the use of good science and decrying the politicizing of the findings. Both those supporting acid rain controls and those opposed to them faulted using science to promote specific policy goals. Members of the electric power industry argued that the science contained in the Interim Assessment clearly demonstrated that acid rain controls were premature and unnecessary at that time. They further asserted that policy makers should wait for the final NAPAP Assessment (due in September of 1990) before instituting any form of controls on acid rain (Hager 1989a, 690).

On the other hand, some scientists and many environmentalists insisted that NAPAP had deliberately softened its findings under pressure from the Reagan administration (Kurtz 1991, A3), even going so far as pronouncing the NAPAP Interim Assessment to be Reagan administration "propaganda" (Hager 1989a, 690). In the end, the political infighting among both scientists and policy makers fostered a very negative image of NAPAP and severely damaged its scientific credibility (Kriz 1990, 895). Simply put, many observers of the policy debate over acid rain feared that the politics of acid rain pollution, as exemplified by the resulting uproar over the release of NAPAP's 1987 Interim Assessment, had rendered the science of acid rain "all but moot" (Hager 1989a, 690).

The 1990 Integrated Assessment Report. The first thing critics often note about the 1990 Integrated Assessment Report is its publication date; November 1991. It was said that by the time the final NAPAP report was released, the major players (Congress, the Bush administration, the utility industry, and the environmental groups) had already cut most of their deals (Kurtz 1991, A3). An editorial in *The New York Times* curtly pointed out that "Political solutions should follow, not precede, scientific conclusions, especially conclusions reached at the cost of $500 million" (1990, A22). Others lamented the inability of policy makers to wait for completion of "the biggest study ever undertaken on acid rain" (Kriz 1990, 896).

The second thing critics note about the final NAPAP assessment is that, like the 1987 Interim Assessment, the 1990 Integrated Assessment underestimated the severity of the acid rain problem. William Stevens reported that some scientists criticized the assessment as prematurely concluding that acid rain was causing little harm to American forests, and that Canadian scientists believed the assessment underestimated the acid rain problem in their country (1990, C1). Of course, others pointed out that the report's findings exposed "the irresponsible hysteria fomented by environmental groups and encouraged in hyperventilating media reports" (Kurtz 1991, A3).

It appears that just as the 1987 Interim Assessment set off a chain of criticism, so did the 1990 Integrated Assessment. In fact, as will be illustrated elsewhere in this book, the entire NAPAP process remains under a cloud of criticism, even today.

Canada and NAPAP. The controversy over the release of the 1987 and 1990 NAPAP reports highlights the fact that much of the debate over the science of acid rain was carried out in the context of a United States–Canada transboundary pollution problem. The struggle to "marshal the best available science to figure out the causes and effects of acid rain and how to control it" (Roberts 1991, 1302) was taken up by scientists in both the United States and Canada, and it was not long before several controversies developed. Furthermore, as delineated in the previous chapter, the argument over scientific uncertainty became the major focus of the transboundary debate over acid rain, with the Canadians calling for immediate action and the United States (i.e., the Reagan administration) insisting that more scientific research was needed before proceeding. The exchanges between Canadian and United States officials during the 1980s clearly show this dichotomy. The Canadian government believed that there was sufficient scientific evidence to act and the United States government did not.

In 1981, Canadian embassy representative George Rejhon stated the official Canadian position: "In our view, there is no doubt that the scientific understanding of the acid rain phenomenon, at this time, both justifies and necessitates the beginning of ameliorative action" (U.S. Congress. House of Representatives. Committee on Science and Technology, Subcommittee on Natural Resources, Agricultural Research and Environment 1981, 382). Anne Gorsuch, director of the United States Environmental Protection Agency at the time, gave the United States reaction to Rejhon's position. "Current parameters of the uncertainty as to the cause and effect [of acid rain], we believe, do not provide a premise for further regulatory action at this time. . . . To conclude at this point that SO_2 equals acid rain is not a conclusion that can be established in the scientific community" (U.S. Congress. House of Representatives. Committee on Energy and Commerce, Subcommittee on Health and the Environment 1982, 284).

In 1983, it was Canadian Environment Minister Roberts who expressed Canada's adamant belief that the scientific evidence supported immediate action: "We have enough information to act. . . . It's not a matter of science any longer, it's a matter of political will. We have reached the point where a decision to only do more research is, in fact, a decision to do nothing" (J. Davis 1983a, 1065). The new director of the United States Environmental Protection Agency, William Ruckelshaus, responded to the Canadian call for action with the following words: "[T]here's no consensus in the country about acid rain. . . . We [have not arrived] at the point where the country is sufficiently convinced that we have a real problem here [with acid rain] that we have to address" (U.S. Congress. House of Representatives. Committee on Science and Technology 1984, 16).

The Canadians again officially reiterated their position in 1985, arguing, "Available scientific information provides a sufficient basis to design and implement [acid rain] abatement programs" (Franklin et al. 1985, 155). But the United States response remained entrenched as Ruckelshaus' replacement at the Environmental Protection Agency, Lee Thomas, argued, "we do not believe that the current state of knowledge can sustain any judgment with respect to the level of emission reductions needed to prevent or eliminate damage from acid rain" (U.S. Congress. Senate. Committee on Energy and Natural Resources 1986, 91).

Throughout the time period of these exchanges, many United States scientific reports appeared to support the Canadian position. The National Academy of Sciences, the Office of Technology Assessment, and the Office of Science and Technology Policy all concluded that the available scientific evidence justified immediate action to control acid rain. In addition, a report published under the auspices of some of the top United States acid rain scientists titled *Is There Scientific Consensus on Acid Rain?* also concluded that there was scientific consensus in many areas and stated that adequate scientific information existed to begin controls (Driscoll et al. 1985). Furthermore, prominent| scientists Dr. Michael Oppenheimer (U.S. Congress. House of Representatives. Committee on Energy and Commerce, Subcommittee on Health and the Environment 1983, 110) and Dr. James Galloway (U.S. Congress. Senate. Committee on Environment and Public Works 1986, 449) as well as respected Congressman Henry Waxman (U.S. Congress. House of Representatives. Committee on Energy and Commerce, Subcommittee on Health and the Environment 1984a, 3) and Senator George Mitchell (U.S. Congress. Senate. Committee on Environment and Public Works 1986, 20) emphatically argued that a scientific consensus existed. Yet, the scientific evidence did not prove compelling enough for policy makers in the United States as a whole to take immediate action to reduce transboundary air pollution.

SCIENTIFIC UNCERTAINTY

As it turned out, those scientists arguing for immediate action to reduce the precursors of acid rain pollution were essentially ignored, at least throughout the decade of the 1980s. The public debate among scientists over whose science was better, the Reagan administration's general response of delay, and the call for more research all provided more than enough uncertainty for policy makers to question the validity of the science (Meyer 1995, B1). Rochelle Stanfield observed that the scientific issues involving acid rain were so complex that both sides of the debate even used the same scientific studies as evidence that they were right (1984, 860) and that the "war of the scientists" came early in the acid rain debate and lingered throughout (1986, 1501).

One prominent acid rain scientist suggested that while acid rain was thought to be a major environmental problem, the scientific evidence "was not sufficiently compelling to overcome the understandable reluctance of Congress to undertake an expensive new regulatory program" (Russell 1992, 107). William Mangun not only supported this point of view but put the blame on both scientists and those who use (misuse) science to their advantage:

Despite overwhelming evidence concerning the causes and consequences of acid rain, scientists [were not] able to convince a sufficient number of Congressmen that the severity of the problem necessitates immediate action in the form of controls on the sources of acid rain. Consequently, there [was no] conversion of scientific data into legislative reform. Part of the difficulty [was] the misinformation campaign waged by the lobbyists for the public utility, coal mining, and manufacturing interest groups (among others) in order to delay the imposition of controls. (1995, 26)

The lack of a genuine scientific consensus with respect to acid rain played a major part in the way that both sides (those who wanted controls, e. g., the Canadians, and those who did not, e. g., the Reagan Administration) approached this debate. Because of the scientific uncertainty surrounding the precise causes and effects of acid rain as they were interpreted by the people who must make the decisions concerning reduction, each side felt free to exercise its own judgment as to what was correct. During the heat of the acid rain debate, the General Accounting Office summarized the effect of scientific uncertainty:

Although science has largely determined that man-made emissions cause acid rain, there is uncertainty concerning the extent and timing of its anticipated effects. Thus, at the present time scientific information alone does not lead unequivocally to a conclusion on whether it is appropriate to begin control actions now or await better understanding. Given this uncertainty, decisionmakers must weigh the risks of further, potentially avoidable environmental damage against the risks of economic impacts from acid rain control actions which may ultimately prove to be unwarranted. (U.S. General Accounting Office 1984, cover)

The confusion and uncertainty surrounding the acid rain debate created a very unflattering picture of science and scientists. Phillip Roeder and Timothy Johnson stated, "A concerned and interested citizen then is unlikely to gain much guidance or to reduce his or her uncertainties on acid rain by analyzing the judgments of scientific experts" (1985, 78). Larry Parker and John Blodgett spoke of "a genuine inadequacy of scientific understanding of the nature of the [acid rain] problem" (1985, 107) and Archie Kahan argued:

Confidence in the ability of science and technology to solve the important environmental problems of the future is not nearly as widespread today as it once was. It has been replaced, in the minds of many people, by the conviction that too much reliance on science and technology has put mankind on a fast track to catastrophe. This diminished confidence in society's ability to cope contributes to the sense of urgency about acid rain. (1986, 8–9)

This inability of science to provide adequate guidance to resolve the policy debate regarding acid rain was summed up by John Gibbons (Director of the Office of Technology Assessment) when he stated that "in OTA's judgment, even substantial additional scientific research is unlikely to provide significant, near-term policy guidance, or resolve value conflicts" (U.S. Office of Technology Assessment 1984, 3).

The role of science (and scientists), as determined by Kingdon (1995, 53–57), Lynn (1986, 48), and Schmandt, Clarkson, and Roderick (1988, 3–4), among others, is to help policy makers assess the seriousness of the problem and to distinguish between technically workable and impractical solutions. In attempting to accomplish this task with respect to the acid rain issue, it appears that scientists often left policy makers in a greater state of confusion, rather than in a position to act.

During the heart of the policy debate, confusion was also pervasive among many of the social scientists and scholars who were closely following (and studying) the acid rain issue. Some thought there existed enough of a scientific consensus to act. Roy Gould suggested, "evidence is massive and convincing that acid rain and related forms of air pollution are taking a serious toll on lakes and streams, forests and soils, water supplies, air quality and human health" and that "the problem has been allowed to fester [too] long" (1985, 123). Archie Kahan revealed that a national survey of 1027 United States acid-deposition researchers suggested that 80 percent of the responding scientists were in favor of immediate and decisive steps to curtail emissions (1986, 158). And Jurgen Schmandt, Judith Clarkson, and Hilliard Rodderick asserted that there was a "solid agreement among experts . . . that burning of fossil fuels was at the root of the acid rain problem in North America" (1988, 15).

On the other hand, some social science researchers doubted that there was enough evidence to convince policy makers to act. Phillip Roeder and Timothy Johnson declared that "a scientific consensus on the causes of acid rain appears to be lacking" (1985, 68) and Randal Ihara contended that scientific understanding about acid rain remained incomplete and that the lack of a scientific consensus made the prospects for a resolution of the acid rain issue "exceedingly problematic" (1985, 20–21).

This confusion over whether a scientific consensus existed or not symbolizes the acid rain policy debate at its worst and highlights the fact that, within the policy process, scientists can only do so much. While scientists were able to bring the acid rain issue to the forefront of the public's attention and even help move the issue onto the governmental agenda, they were at great disadvantage once the issue was framed within a policy (political) context. Scientists found out that policy makers wanted much more than just the scientific facts; they wanted advice on exactly what they should do. Scientists who offered such advice (like Rahn) were castigated for politicizing the science. Scientists who refused to offer such advice (like Cowling and Galloway) were left to defend their position and explain why they should not be asked to provide their personal opinions. At least from the experience of the acid rain debate that took place in the halls of Congress, it appears that scientists and policy makers do not understand (or want to understand) each others' language or forms of communication.

Furthermore, policy makers who are resistant to change can (and do) use the confusion between the scientific and political worlds to their advantage. For (as illustrated above) scientific uncertainty favors not acting. If the science is not definitive, which is almost always the case, then policy makers can take cover behind the call to wait for more science. Scientists have a difficult time overcoming this situation because the very essence of their world is uncertainty and they are required to speak in those terms. Hence, by framing the debate in the political world (as opposed to the scientific world) there will always be questions about the science. This was certainly true with respect to the acid rain issue.

QUESTIONS ABOUT THE SCIENCE OF ACID RAIN

Despite the apparent success of establishing controls on acid rain pollution (as signified by the signing of the 1990 Clean Air Act Amendments and the approval of the Air Quality Accord), the value of science (and scientists) to the policy-making process that led to this success has been seriously questioned. As illustrated at the beginning of this book, it has been asserted that scientists involved in the development of a United States acid rain policy got classified as supporting one side or the other of the policy debate, because advocates from all sides attempted to use the science to support their own policy-making efforts or disparage those of their opponents (Lackey and Blair 1997, 9). Worse yet, it has been suggested by Orie Loucks that the obvious misuse of science during the acid rain debate has led to the loss of a substantial measure of prestige for United States scientists, even to the point where United States science is perceived by the international scientific community as seriously lacking in credibility (1993, 72).

In a series of articles carried in *Power Engineering*, Ralph Perhac (the former director of the Environmental Science Department of the Electric Power

Research Institute) asked, "Why did science, which is such an important part of the acid rain issue, seem to have such a small influence in the legislative process?" (1991a, 38). Perhac made a scathing attack on the use of science and the role that scientists played in the development of the United States policy on transboundary pollution. He accused individual scientists of acting out of self-interest, using hyperbole and selective data to support policy positions, and even of outright advocation of policy positions without clearly distinguishing between policy and science. Perhac further faulted the utility industry for putting "too much faith in science as a means of resolving a complex scientific/political issue" like acid rain (1991b, 26).

Perhac's focus was the scientific work produced by the National Acid Precipitation Assessment Program and its relationship to the final policy outcome. Perhac maintained that because few policy makers are trained in science, it is unrealistic to expect them to judge the value of testimonies (even if given by reputable scientists) that contain more opinionated debate than fact. Perhac also noted that politics moves faster than science and that complex scientific uncertainties cannot be resolved in the time frame needed by elected officials (1991a, 38–40; 1991b, 26–29).

These same ideas (that the science of acid rain was corrupted by politics and that science must somehow be separated from policy judgments) are also reflected in a series of *Ecological Applications* articles about the acid rain issue written by some of the most prominent North American scientists involved in the development of the science of transboundary air pollution. The evaluations and critiques of the science of acid rain provided by these scientists (from both Canada and the United States) offer a unique and important perspective on the current state of the science-policy linkage. Some of these scientists viewed the science-policy linkage (as exemplified by NAPAP) in a very derogatory light. For instance, David Schindler (1992, 124) felt that the search for a North American solution to transboundary air pollution included deliberate political interference with the course of science and delays in the release of first-rate science that did not support political agendas. He cited examples of first-class American scientists being virtually isolated because they would not conform to political objectives and detailed instances that, he felt, led to the obfuscation of scientific conclusions.

Some scientists used the articles in *Ecological Applications* to comment on the way science should be conducted. Among these scientists was Ellis Cowling, who proclaimed that the responsibility of scientists in a democracy is to understand and clearly communicate the scientific facts and uncertainties and to describe expected outcomes objectively (1992, 113–14). Cowling also argued that the proper role for scientists is to provide advice and counsel to those who are charged by our society with making policy decisions, rather than make societal decisions or even try to have special influence on those societal decisions. Along similar lines, Milton Russell felt that environmental scientists should be isolated from influence over what they find and report and that the only way to insure the integrity of this effort is by careful adherence to the canons of the scientific process, including peer review (1992, 108).

Questions about how science should eventually be linked to the policy-making process remain important and worthy of study. Moreover, because scientists (and science) have come under such intense criticism in policy debates over such environmental concerns as acid rain, it is meaningful to investigate how scientists perceive their ties to the policy world. The purpose of the next chapter is to do just that.

NOTES

1. Indeed, some credit the scientific work completed by the National Atmospheric Deposition Program (NADP) in the 1970s with prompting President Jimmy Carter to recognize acid rain as a serious environmental problem deserving of attention at the highest levels of government (U.S. Congress. House of Representatives. Committee on Interstate and Foreign Commerce, Subcommittee on Oversight and Investigations, 1980, 148–49).

2. While Smith first used the term "acid rain" in his book, *Air and Rain: The Beginnings of a Chemical Climatology* in 1872, he had detailed many of the features of the acid rain phenomenon twenty years earlier in a report about the chemistry of rain in and around the city of Manchester, England (Cowling 1982, 111A).

3. Gene Likens of Cornell University is generally given credit for being the person who first gave prominence to the acid precipitation problem in the United States (Kerr 1982, 881).

4. During this time period, as reported in the *Congressional Quarterly Weekly*, Russell Peterson (Audubon Society president and former Republican governor of Delaware and chairman of the Council on Environmental Quality) charged the Reagan administration with becoming increasingly reliant on outside science and showing "contempt for independent scientists who bring information which is inconsistent with the administration's political agenda" (J. Davis 1982b, 1829).

5. In the final analysis, Reagan's position on the 1987 NAPAP interim report suffered a severe setback. When Dr. James Mahoney, the new Director of NAPAP, testified before Congress the year after the report was released, he conceded that the executive summary could be more representative of the full body of scientific information and he agreed to provide an appropriate new summary (U.S. Congress. House of Representatives. Committee on Science, Space and Technology, Subcommittee on Natural Resources, Agricultural Research and Environment 1988, 46).

6. During the 1980s (as was depicted earlier), Dingell and Senate Majority leader Robert Byrd (both Democrats representing constituencies opposed to acid rain legislation) led the opposition to acid rain controls in the U.S. Congress. Along with President Ronald Reagan in the White House, these leaders proved to be a very powerful (if informal) coalition against those who were pushing for action to reduce transboundary air pollution (Bryner 1995; R. Cohen 1995).

Chapter 5

Scientists, Policy Makers, and Acid Rain

INTRODUCTION

One of the goals of this book is to highlight an often-ignored view of the policy process: that of scientists. With that in mind, this and the following chapter will present the views of scientists on the science-policy linkage. Scientists were asked to respond to large philosophical questions about the importance of science to environmental policy making and about the difficulty of remaining true to the canons (such as objectivity) of the scientific process. Each chapter begins with a review of the scholarly literature related to the specific questions asked of the scientists and ends with a discussion of what the scientists said in reply.

A QUESTION OF SCIENTIFIC RELEVANCE

As introduced in Chapter 1 and as documented in the last chapter, when the policy debate in the United States over acid rain came to an official conclusion with the passage of the Clean Air Act Amendments in late 1990 and the signing (with Canada) of the Air Quality Accord in early 1991, a series of articles published in scholarly journals were severely critical of the role that science and scientists had played in the formulation of this policy. One set of charges centered on the idea that the science of acid rain was essentially irrelevant to the policy process. Simply put, the charge was made that policy makers either ignored the good science that was produced or chose to consider only the science (and scientists) that supported their previously established political ideologies. Along these lines, there were specific charges of political interference with the course of science and delays in the release of first-rate science because it was not supportive of particular political agendas.

Furthermore, both policy makers and scientists alike were accused of failing to keep scientific facts separate from political values.

A second set of charges centered on the scientists themselves and on the idea that, during the acid rain debate, many scientists abandoned the tenets of the scientific method (including objectivity) in an effort to directly influence the policy (political) process. In essence, acid rain scientists were charged with using selective science to advocate specific policies that would benefit them both professionally and personally.

The articles noted above were written by some of the most respected and prestigious scientists in the United States and Canada, who were deeply involved in acid rain research over a long period of time. Their criticism was directed specifically at the science of acid rain and the scientists who were doing acid rain research. Yet, according to other scholars and scientists, their complaints went far beyond a singular focus on acid rain. They represented a growing concern about the science-policy linkage in general. As Charles Enman observed: "Science wants to conduct an impartial search for the truth. Bureaucracy searches for policy to fit myriad objectives, only some of which answer to scientific considerations. How, then, can science and bureaucracy peacefully coexist" (1997, B1)?

TWO DIFFERENT WORLDS: POLICY MAKERS AND SCIENTISTS

William Leiss believes that two unifying themes run through all the various battles over the best approach to environmental policy making in North America: the use of science as a justification for action (or inaction) and the question of scientific credibility (Leiss 1996, 124). In addressing these themes, Leiss differentiated between using science as the primary driver of environmental policy making and using science as a primary component of environmental policy making.[1] The reasons why Leiss believes that such a differentiation exists are straightforward: (1) Environmental policy requires yes or no decisions, whereas science often is continually evolving from one level of uncertainty to another; (2) In a political context, environmental policy making is often driven by just those issues for which there exists the most imperfect scientific understanding; and (3) Environmental issues usually lack immediacy in that they are based on long-term trends, whereas, in the total context of government policy making, economic, jurisdictional, political, legal and other factors have a stark immediacy that simply cannot be overlooked by politicians (Leiss 1996, 125).

Within this context, Leiss referred to the constant refrain that good environmental policies must be rooted in good science, meaning that issues about environmental protection should be based on a thorough understanding of the leading edge of published scientific research findings (1996, 125). Leiss also argued that a tendency exists for science to become entangled in the policy conflict in such a way that scientists drop their primary focus of actually doing research and get drawn into protracted policy warfare, eventually performing functions for which they have had no decent training or experiential background

(1996, 126). Leiss suggests that because scientists and policy makers function in two different worlds, policy competence (i.e., the ability to find ways to defeat institutional barriers to needed changes in our ways of doing business) is independent of scientific competence (1996, 127).

Leiss's contentions have found support among other noted environmental scholars. For example, Walter Rosenbaum has also found substantial differences between scientists and policy makers, especially with respect to what policy makers want and scientists can produce (1998, 125–30). According to Rosenbaum, policy makers want accurate and credible data and they want it immediately. Yet, scientists often cannot produce this type of information in a timely manner, if at all. In fact, Rosenbaum reported that environmental policies are often made (and unmade) without resort to the scientific evidence that is supposed to govern such decisions. More important, just as Leiss described in his work, Rosenbaum found that environmental issues draw public officials and scientists into a treacherous zone between science and politics that compels public officials to make scientific judgments and scientists to resolve policy issues when neither has been trained to do so (1998, 126).

Other scholars, however, have rejected the notion that such a straightforward dichotomous linkage between science and politics or between scientists and policy makers exists. Karen Litfin, for instance, portrayed a more complex policy world in which knowledge and power must be understood as interactive and where science and politics function together in a multidimensional way (1994, 184). Litfin made the case that it is scientific knowledge, rather than the scientists themselves, that proves crucial to environmental policy making; that is, once scientific knowledge is produced, it becomes available for a host of political actors to exploit in ways that promote certain policies (1994, 188). Essentially, Litfin believes,

[s]cientists may join together in an epistemic community to influence the course of policy. . . . Their power is circumscribed by a host of contextual factors. Policymakers may co-opt or manipulate the scientists, or they may simply ignore what the scientists have to say. Whether or not the voices of scientists are audible may depend upon seemingly extraneous contingencies beyond the control of either scientists or policymakers. Furthermore, the scientists may deliberately refrain from addressing the policy implications of their research. (1994, 188)

But it is in her description of how scientists involved in the debate over stratospheric ozone were drawn out of their laboratories and into the negotiation process that Litfin has touched on the most controversial aspect of a scientist's linkage to public policy making: whether scientists can provide reliable and ideologically neutral data to policy makers (1994, 187). John Zillman characterized this aspect of the science-policy debate as "the challenge that the quickening pace of policy formulation poses to the objectivity of science" (1997, 1084). Along these lines, Bruce Smith talked about the mystique and prestige of science in providing political legitimacy, and characterized science as helping "to legitimate policy by defining the boundaries of the technically feasible and the politically acceptable" (1992, 202). Essentially (as viewed by Ingram, Milward, and Laird) the value of science to government is seen "not primarily in the truth of what scientists say, but in the legitimacy they provide" (1990, 11).

Even with this said, the prevailing view among scholars appears to be that science (and scientists) cannot provide the sort of legitimacy that actors in the policy process crave (Collingridge and Reeve 1986, 158). For instance, Sheila Jasanoff contended that both empirical and theoretical research have effectively dismantled the idea that the scientific component of decision making can be separated from the political component and entrusted to independent experts (1990, 16). Furthermore, in an article, "Environmental Science Under Siege in the U.S. Congress," George E. Brown Jr. [the ranking Democratic member of the House Committee on Science at the time of these statements] served notice that concerns about the existence of good science are still a very real part of our present-day environmental policy-making process. Brown painted a picture in which policy makers have dismissed "the scientific viewpoint established through rigorous peer review in favor of an untested scientific viewpoint whose only benefit [is] that it [supports] a preferred policy outcome" (1997, 19).

The culprits in this move away from good science are the skeptical scientists who have rejected the conventional wisdom of valid scientific analysis and chosen instead to present their views in opinion pieces aimed at policy makers, the media, and the general public rather than their fellow scientists (G. Brown 1997, 15). The way to combat this tendency of policy makers to move away from good science, according to Brown, is for the scientific community to invest a much greater amount of time and energy in educating policy makers and the public about the importance and value of the scientific process, including peer review (1997, 20–21).

This suggestion—that the solution to making the science-policy linkage more effective lies in the education of policy makers (and the public) by scientists— has received a good amount of attention recently. Gretchen Daily proclaimed that the lack of understanding of the character and value of natural ecosystems traces ultimately to a failure of the scientific community to effectively convey the necessary information to the public (1997, xv). Jasanoff spoke of an unspoken presumption that better scientific characterization of a problem will lead to better policy (1990, 7). And Jane Gregory and Steve Miller have contended that, within the last decade, scientists have been delivered a new commandment from on high: to communicate with the public about their work (1998, 1).

SCIENTISTS' PERCEPTIONS OF THE SCIENCE-POLICY LINKAGE

As illustrated above and in the previous chapters, scholars, policy makers, and even scientists themselves have questioned the effectiveness of the science-policy linkage. This was particularly true with the acid rain issue. Policy makers were accused of not only ignoring what scientists had to say, but of politicizing the good science that they did receive. Scientists were condemned for advocating specific policy solutions and for not maintaining an acceptable separation from the politics of acid rain. In essence, scientists were accused of failing to follow the professional standards encompassed by the tenets of the scientific process, especially as these standards call for scientists to remain objective in completing their research.

Essentially, there are three criticisms of the science-policy linkage as it involves environmental policy making. First is the question of how much influence scientists have on environmental policy decisions. In the case of acid rain, the criticism has been that scientists played a very small role and that, ultimately, science had little influence on the final policy-making decisions. Much was made of the fact that the most comprehensive and important scientific report on acid rain was not published until after the policy decisions on acid rain had already been made. Second, because scientists and policy makers operate in two different worlds, the expectation is that science and policy (politics) will seldom coalesce. It has been pointed out that the time frames each of these professions work within are essentially different; that is, policy makers need and want instantaneous solutions and scientists are restricted by the fact that science evolves over long periods of time and always under the cloud of uncertainty. Third, there is a general belief that science is corrupted by politics. Because of this corruption, it has been posited that science should be separated from politics (and policy making) and that scientists should be protected from political influence. This view supports the notion that scientists should not become entangled in the policy world. Instead, science is supposed to provide legitimacy for policy decisions, with scientists providing objective advice and counsel to policy makers without attempting to influence the actual decisions.

The interviews conducted for this study provided a forum for acid rain scientists to express their opinions about these criticisms of the science-policy linkage. The natural scientists interviewed for this study participated directly in research dealing with acid rain. Among other activities, they published the results of their research in both peer-reviewed journals and popular outlets, testified at both congressional hearings and general public hearings, and served on advisory committees and joint United States and Canadian research bodies. The social scientists interviewed for this study did not necessarily participate directly (as the natural scientists did) in the acid rain debate itself. However, they were observers of the environmental policy-making process as it related to both acid rain and to the general influence of science (and scientists) on environmental policy making. Those interviewed for this study came from both the United States and Canada.[2]

One hundred and twenty nine scientists participated in this study. They were asked to respond to four broad, philosophical, and open-ended questions: Do policy makers listen to scientists? Is it possible to separate science from policy making? Should scientists advocate policy positions? Is it possible for scientists to be objective? The first two of these questions are the subject of this chapter and the latter two are the subject of the following chapter.

The answers to these questions shed light on how both natural scientists involved in acid rain research and social scientists involved in observing (studying) the evolution of a North American acid rain policy agreement view the science-policy linkage. The answers also provide a glimpse into the similarities and differences between the perceptions of United States and Canadian scientists.

The Influence of Science

Interpretation of Table 5.1. One of the major criticisms of environmental policy making (and of acid rain policy making in particular) is that scientists' influence is minimal and that policy is often made without sufficient scientific input. The answers (summarized in Table 5.1) to the interview question, "Do policy makers listen to scientists?" appeared to bear out this criticism. Overall, the scientists interviewed for this study agreed with many of the published criticisms of the science-policy linkage as they apply to the acid rain issue and to environmental policy making in general. The majority view among the interviewed scientists (75%; n=97) was that science (and scientists) do not wield a great deal of influence on policy makers. Furthermore, there was a substantial amount of skepticism among these scientists about policy makers and the policy process. Most maintained that the world of policy making is dominated by political considerations and, hence, science plays a subordinate and supplementary role.

It is also interesting to note that some differences exist between natural scientists and social scientists as well as between United States scientists and Canadian scientists with respect to the influence of science. In the United States, natural scientists were clearly the most skeptical about the influence of science. Four of the United States natural scientists (and one of the Canadian natural scientists) stated that policy makers do not listen to scientists at all. To have even one natural scientist imply that scientists have *no* influence on the policy-making process seems quite amazing, given the scientific complexity of our environmental problems today.

The interview results suggest that there are some differences between United States and Canadian perceptions. In Canada, the relationship between the type of scientist and his or her perception of the influence of science is just the opposite of that relationship in the United States. In Canada, it is the social scientists that appear more skeptical of scientific influence. Only four (13%) of the interviewed Canadian social scientists asserted that scientists have a strong influence on policy makers. On the other hand, ten (30%) of the interviewed Canadian natural scientists submitted that scientists provide a strong influence on policy makers.

What Respondents Said. Actual comments from those interviewed provide special insight into how scientists view the impact of science on policy making. Respondents who supported the view that scientists have a strong influence on policy makers spoke of "a reverence for scientists among policy makers," of policy makers being "intimidated by the science," and of policy makers acting as if the science "came from God." [3] A seemingly more realistic view was given by a Canadian social scientist:

Table 5.1
Scientists' Perceptions of Policy Makers

The interview question was: "Do policy makers listen to scientists?"

PART A: Number of answers given by category (as coded by author)

	United States		Canada	
	Natural Scientists (n=33)	Social Scientists (n=32)	Natural Scientists (n=33)	Social Scientists (n=31)
Scientists provide a strong influence on policy makers	2	9	10	4
Scientists provide a moderate to weak influence on policy makers	25	23	22	27
Policy makers do not listen to scientists	4	0	1	0
Do not know	2	0	0	0

PART B: Comments (by number of times cited)

	United States		Canada	
	Natural Scientists (n=33)	Social Scientists (n=32)	Natural Scientists (n=33)	Social Scientists (n=31)
Communications problems exist between scientists and policy makers	12	4	9	8
Policy makers listen when results are politically palatable to them	11	13	6	10
Policy makers do not listen to scientists	1	4	3	8

Source: Author's Computation.

Policy makers listen to scientists more than any other producers of knowledge. Scientists are fairly privileged in the policy discourse. Even if policy makers really don't listen to the scientists much, they listen to them more than [to] any other possessors of knowledge. It is a matter of political expediency.

For the most part though, the respondents saw the influence of science as quite marginal. Comments such as "policy makers listen but don't always take into account the scientific information as much as scientists would wish" and "policy makers have many other things to consider besides science" suggested that many of the respondents view science as only one part of the decision-making process. A United States natural scientist (first quote) and a Canadian natural scientist (second quote) gave two typical responses:

A lot of scientists like to think science is the only foundation of decisions. I think of policy decisions as a pie and scientists get their slice and it is real important that you provide the best science you can for your slice. It is unreasonable to base policy solely on science. There are many other impacts like distribution and equity and it is totally unreasonable for scientists to address these issues.

For policy makers it is a juggling act. They have many things to consider besides science. My view as a scientist is that they pay me so I give it my best shot and then go about my business. It is not a case of policy makers not listening but of them making trade-offs and scientists getting lost amongst other issues.

Another Canadian natural scientist put it this way:

Policy makers have constraints that scientists don't have. The question is not whether they listen but if they implement what they hear. Scientists and policy makers have different functions. Policy makers have a broader group to satisfy. They listen, but most of the time they don't do what scientists say.

Two Different Worlds

As described earlier, a major criticism of environmental policy making is that scientists have difficulty making the connection with policy makers because scientists and policy makers operate in two completely different contexts; neither are trained to understand the others' point of view. For instance, policy makers are viewed as wanting certainty (yes/no answers) and immediate solutions, while science takes time to evolve and scientists deal only in the realm of uncertainty. Along these lines, many scholars (and critics of the acid rain policy process) also believe that because of the differences between their respective fields of expertise, scientists and policy makers have difficulty hearing what each other have to say.

Another common criticism of the science-policy linkage is that politics corrupts science. In this regard, many scientists (and scholars) call for the protection of scientists from the influence of policy makers (politics). They submit that scientists should be allowed to operate separately from the political world so that they can provide good scientific advice and counsel to those who have to make the policy decisions.

Interpretation of Table 5.2. The results of the interview question "Is it possible to separate science from policy making?" listed in Table 5.2 suggest that while many of these criticisms are commonly perceived by those interviewed, differences exist between how natural scientists and social scientists view the science-policy linkage. In the United States and Canada, a much larger percentage of natural scientists (68%; n=45) than social scientists (44%; n=28) said that it is possible to separate science from policy. In addition, comments from the interviewees implied that there is a strong belief among scientists that in today's world, science must be policy relevant, and that science is inherently based within a political dialogue because scientific research is so dependent on outside funding (both public and private).

What Respondents Said. The case for separating science from policy was made predominantly by natural scientists along the following lines:

It is possible for scientists to avoid considering policy and study pollution as a fundamental science. That is what I do and I would be insulted if someone called me an applied scientist. Now, policy makers cannot make policy without scientists, but it is possible for scientists to do science without policy and policy makers.

When policy makers make decisions, they make them with filtered information. It is a complicated process. But policy makers are very busy and have no time to read actual scientific reports. They read an executive summary after it has first been prepared by scientists who summarize, and then interim people who simplify. By the time it gets to the powers that be, they only get a flavor of the original science, which they never see. So the issue has been graded down three times removed from the original data.

Other natural scientists thought it was possible, but not desirable to separate science from policy.

It is possible but not desirable to totally separate science from policy. It is like Milton Russell says: "semipermeable barriers." There needs to be a point of communication and discussion. But the functions need to be clearly stated up front, what is appropriate and inappropriate. Lay out the policy questions. Policy makers must do that to engage the scientists who need to understand what the question is. Once this is done so the scientist knows the question and the policy maker knows the limitations of science, then the science can be separated from the policy maker and the science can be done objectively.

The case was also made (predominantly by social scientists) that there could never be a separation of science from policy.

The entire notion of separating science from policy is absurd.

It is abundantly clear that science has political implications. Science is not neutral. There is no such thing as neutral knowledge. Science is political, with its funding, choices of topics, how knowledge is dispersed, and the involvement of scientists in the policy process. Science is political and politics is scientific.

Table 5.2
Scientists' Perceptions of Separation of Science and Policy

The interview question was: "Is it possible to separate science from policy making?"

PART A: Number of answers given by category (as coded by author)

	United States		Canada	
	Natural Scientists (n=33)	Social Scientists (n=32)	Natural Scientists (n=33)	Social Scientists (n=31)
Yes	22	15	23	13
No	11	17	10	18

PART B: Comments (by number of times cited)

	United States		Canada	
	Natural Scientists (n=33)	Social Scientists (n=32)	Natural Scientists (n=33)	Social Scientists (n=31)
All science is policy-relevant	8	4	5	2
All science is subsumed by politics	4	4	3	7
A need exists for a liason between scientists and policy makers	2	4	3	5
The science-policy linkage is subsumed by the influence of money	3	5	3	1

Source: Author's Computation.

Both science and policy making are located in a broader puddle. They are part of an overall culture where normative ideas are good, real, and possible. But we still have political expediency. There's a certain kind of research that is funded and certain policies are supported. Science and policy are tied together in this culture.

Respondents were particularly inclined to talk about the difference between scientists and policy makers. The idea that scientists and policy makers function in two different worlds and speak two different languages came up time and again during the interviews. One United States social scientist described the science-policy linkage this way:

Policy makers do listen because they value and want factual information based on scientific studies. The problem is that because of the nature of the discipline, scientists tend to hedge their findings. Policy makers want a right or wrong answer and scientists cannot give that. Policy makers want yes or no answers and they get frustrated because they are under time constraints.

A Canadian natural scientist observed that:

Scientists and policy makers function in two entirely different value systems in thinking and behavior. One system is science and one is politics. To practitioners in each world, their world is rational and the worlds do not overlap and neither is particularly interested in the rules of the other. It is "wonky" scientists or political "hacks." Both believe they have insight and that they possess the absolute truth. They each possess egos of monumental proportions. Practitioners in both systems are egocentric and tend to be dismissive of the other party. They don't understand each other.

The idea that scientists and policy makers speak two different languages was also prevalent among those interviewed.

The problem is that scientists and policy makers do not talk the same language. It is very difficult to communicate with each other. They talk in different spatial scales. Scientists are just different.

Remember that policy makers and scientists work on two different time scales. Policy changes by the week and typically in science, five years is a short time for change to occur. We need some type of synthesis, a rule book where a policy maker understands what works and what doesn't. We need to work out something like a marriage contract. Both sides need to understand the rules.

There must be a linkage between science and policy. The problem is when we get scientists trying to be policy makers and policy makers trying to be scientists. Both are amateurs in the other's field.

The skills are just not there for each side to dabble in the other side. If scientists come up with the right answer then there has to be a better way of communicating the right answer. There are inadequacies on both sides and real large deficiencies on both sides. "Mr. Ph.D." gives the information but it doesn't answer the question because he doesn't know what the policy maker wants.

Many of the respondents spoke of the poor communication linkages between scientists and policy makers. A United States natural scientist submitted:

It's just a matter of communication. Science is just not getting through. Policy makers and scientists have different approaches to the problem in terms of what scientists can produce and what policy makers need. Either it is not the right information or not in the right form.

Many respondents blamed the policy makers.

Policy makers have no sense to judge good or bad science. Policy makers are selective, predisposed, and want certainty and scientists cannot give them that.

Policy makers view scientists as naive fools, having their proverbial heads in the sand, not having any idea what the real world is about, sequestered in their own special place.

Policy makers want input but they are ill equipped to deal with the input when they get it. But policy makers do it because the public believes scientists and policy makers know that. No one has higher credibility than scientists do.

Policy makers do not listen to scientists very carefully and yes, it bothers me. Policy makers are not sufficiently aware of what they are asking. I view most policy makers as being disciplined in the law and there is a complete disconnect between scientists and lawyers. Lawyers base things on precedent where there are absolutes. There are no absolutes in science. Science is always tentative and subject to revision. It is very hard for non-technical people to grasp.

You have to talk to policy makers for a long time and the evidence has to be clear and unambiguous. You can't be saying "On the one hand this and on the other hand this." As Ed Muskie said so clearly, what policy makers want are one-armed scientists.

Policy makers look in your eyes and have their ears open and write things down. But there is a real question about their comprehension. They say all the good things to you but when all is said and done, I suspect that the vast majority of policy makers miss the vast majority of what scientists have to say.

However, a good many of the natural scientists also blamed themselves.

Scientists talk about uncertainty and use "weasel words" that are often seized by [one] side of the issue as indicating grave doubts.

Scientists are their own worst enemy. In general, the entire profession has long basked in the notion that we are separate, above the common folk. And even if I take the time to talk and explain it to you in laymen's terms, you're too stupid or you will twist what I'm saying to fit your perspective because I'm credible.

Those interviewed for this study also emphasized that the key to making the connection between science and policy lies in how scientists approach the policy makers. There was a general belief that policy makers were not making the effort to bring these two worlds together and that if the connection is going to be made, it has to come at the urging of scientists. It was submitted that because policy makers do not understand "this mysterious scientific language," scientists must make sure their presentations are completed "in such a way that policy makers can understand." Further, several respondents said that getting policy makers to listen was dependent upon how skillful scientists were in articulating the policy-relevant science. As one United States natural scientist maintained:

If you approach policy makers correctly and can speak to them on their terms and put things in context, in their context, then they will listen.

Another United States natural scientist put the burden of communication squarely on scientists.

When scientists articulate the policy-relevant science in a meaningful way, policy makers listen. It is a matter of how skillful the scientists are in presenting their material. It is a matter of scientists packaging the science in a way that makes sense to policy makers. I hate to have to say that, but it is a matter of putting it in these terms.

Many respondents thought that improving communications would increase the chances that good science would make it to the policy maker. They called for increased communications between scientists and policy makers and for the establishment of a formal feedback loop.

If science is to be relevant to people there needs to be a feedback loop right at the beginning of the process so that policy makers can frame what scientists should address. There is always a lot of focus on [communication from] science to policy and less emphasis on the reverse route.

The separation of science and policy should be a goal to work toward. There ought to be a lot of communication between scientists and policy makers both from scientists to policy makers and policy makers to scientists. Policy makers provide the area of interest and the purse strings. Scientists say what they are finding. But the two roles should be separated. In an ideal world you should keep them as separate as you can.

To have a functional system you need feedback loops that accurately and on a timely basis give information back to the other side. Science provides the data and policy makers the questions. The question is in degrees of overlap. There still needs to be a way to insulate the sides. But there is more of an effort from the policy side to influence the science side than the other way around. Scientific integrity must be protected from the policy imperative of the day.

Many respondents also maintained that a need exists for more people who can bridge the gap between the policy side and the science side, people who have training in both worlds.

It is possible to separate science from policy as long as there is a liaison person who can translate between the two, an individual who understands science and can translate scientific information that is useful to the policy maker. Most scientists cannot do that or don't do that well. They are caught up in their research and don't think about the policy aspects.

There is a need to have knowledge brokers in the middle that will interpret the science and scientific findings, to consolidate the science and express it in a policy-relevant manner. The science needs to be useful and it is necessary to explain it to policy makers.

For some, the future looks bleak for resolving the communication linkage between scientists and policy makers. As a Canadian social scientist asserted:

The interface of science and policy is the single most important dilemma that we have. We are still making decisions without science because the interface is so impoverished. The science-policy linkage is problematic. I don't think that anybody has even taken as a task to try and define the notion of an interface and, hence, this linkage is problematic. The problem is with the interface itself. It exists and is recognized as such and many of the policy choices are based on science. But in many cases the interface is rough and arbitrary and doesn't work very well. I don't think there is a sorting out between the notion of science and other things. It is not very sensible.

Another view that was pervasive among the interviewees was that policy makers listen to scientists only when it fits their personal agendas or when the scientific evidence is "politically palatable." A United States natural scientist summarized this view:

Policy makers only listen to scientists when it is in their interest to do so and under two circumstances: one, if the scientist promotes ideas that support the policy maker's preconceived notions and two, if the policy maker is being pressed by public opinion. That is what drives policy makers. They might consult for help in coming up with remedies consistent with their position and public opinion, but it is very rare that policy makers pay a great deal of attention to what scientists say.

One other United States natural scientist put it this way:

Yes, policy makers listen but they have agendas of their own and their level of listening reflects their personal biases. If they find scientists who agree with their preconceived notions then they become their champion and seek to minimize, and are critical of, anyone who disagrees.

Many of those interviewed not only felt that "the bulk of science goes unheard," but also took what they perceived as policy makers' indifference very personally. One United States natural scientist described his participation on a panel that was briefing the director of the Environmental Protection Agency with respect to acid rain controls:

When it came to me, his [EPA Director] eyes glazed over and it was like isn't that nice but I can't wait to get on to the next person. I was a minority of one and no one in D.C., corporations, or at universities was doing what I was doing and no one is going to listen to a minority of one because historically speaking minorities of one are wrong. So how do you counteract that? You spend your entire life fighting that. I was trying to make a contribution but didn't realize the dynamics and odds I was up against.

Another United States natural scientist expressed his frustration:

Other countries do a better job of listening to the scientists than we do in the United States. During the early part of the acid rain debate a group of half ecologists and half environmentalists and policy makers got together for a one-day workshop. There were six or seven scientists and we decided to pull all the available scientific information into one report. We did not include one word of our own research. All we did was look at major research that had already been completed and look for answers there. We did that and formalized that into a report titled *Is There Scientific Consensus on Acid Rain?* and we distributed that report everywhere—to policy makers, to environmentalists, to industry, all over—and guess what? It had no impact whatsoever. Zero! And some of the research reports we studied were inches thick. We took the view, let the research speak for itself and it would be powerful. It was not.

Respondents also made many references to the penchant of policy makers to "shop" for scientists that support their particular ideological views and for policy makers of different views to use "dueling scientists." One United States natural scientist explained it in terms of policy makers legitimizing what they already believed.

The EPA asked us to do a technical analysis and it was clear from the beginning that they had the answer they wanted and wanted us to justify that answer. They wanted to hear but got concerned if [what we said] deviated from expectations.

Others argued that the fault for such gross politicization of the science lay with the failure of the scientific community to develop consensus opinions. One United States social scientist said that:

Because scientists cannot agree, and that is the nature of the scientific method, the policy makers just choose to listen to the ones that support their point of view.

Another United States social scientist put it this way:

Policy makers pay attention to the science that tells them things that are consistent with their beliefs and goals and not to others. There is always enough variation in the science and scientists that they can find someone to tell them what they want.

Many respondents cast this linkage as one dominated by politics.

What you are really asking is whether you can separate science from values and I'd say that is pretty damn hard. The choice of data, method, everything is influential. Very few scientists do not have a political view of the science they are doing. It is tied to financing and money. If there is no uncertainty, then you can separate. If there is great uncertainty, you cannot separate because how you feel about the uncertainties tells you how you act.

Some scientists are stuck back in 1755 with their attitudes. They are technicians and believe you can have it separate and objective and don't realize the entire system is political.

There is no science that remains untouched by politics. The question is, what is science doing for society? This is a public question, a legitimate question, part of the culture. What is science doing for society as a whole?

Other respondents talked about the political arena in the context of providing the necessary monetary resources for scientific research to be successful.

At the highest level there are relatively few projects undertaken under simple naive curiosity. This should be encouraged, but there are relatively few. Most scientists applying for money are stimulated by the public and it is in the political arena, whether the scientists know it or not. Any project is driven by the dollars and for political reasons. These projects, right from the beginning, are political. Scientists may not think they are, but they are.

How we decide to make decisions and allocate dollars is in our political system. Science only comes into play after the political decision is made as to what the outcome is supposed to be and that is political.

It is perfectly possible to separate science from policy. Scientific study can be completely isolated, assuming you can get the dollars.

Science must be protected against manipulation. We must be careful about how science and policy interact. Because such large amounts of money are required it is not even possible to separate science from policy.

The idea that science should be more closely linked to societal concerns was also mentioned frequently in the interviews.

If I gave you $1 million to study what interests you, then you can have no connection. Clearly, you can do that. But the minute justifications are rooted in societal concerns, then you cannot separate. We used to do that with philanthropists in the twentieth century. But no more. Research is expected to be for the public good. It is societal now and you must make the connection.

We really erode our political and public policy dialogue if we think of social policy in separate compartments. Science clearly has to focus on the majority policy questions. Yet, most scientists don't know how to phrase the question or organize their research to answer the question. There is a continuum of communication that is stronger today compared to twenty years ago. Natural scientists have much more difficulty understanding that the policy process is not static and policy people have trouble understanding the dynamics of the natural systems.

Because policy provides the resources, today much of what science does is driven by society's view of what is important rather than trying to research and provide a thorough understanding of how the world works. Science and policy are not independent. Science is steered by the availability of resources.

It is possible to separate science from policy but that is a waste of money because it won't pass the "So what?" test. Science must be policy-relevant.

You must always think in terms of policy outcomes rather than pure science. It is useless to know the solution and not be able to use it. Then science becomes useless. You must connect it.

SUMMARY OF INTERVIEW FINDINGS

Only a small percentage of the scientists interviewed expressed the view that scientists provide a strong influence on policy makers. The vast majority supported the view that scientists, at best, provide a moderate to weak influence on policy makers. United States natural scientists appeared to be the most skeptical of the influence of science, although Canadian social scientists also appeared quite skeptical. The tabular results also indicated that United States respondents are more apt to view the science-policy linkage in political terms and that within the United States, a much larger number of natural scientists than social scientists see serious problems with communication between scientists and policy makers.

With respect to the question of separation of science and policy, no United States–Canadian differences appeared substantial. However, an apparent difference does exist between the perceptions of natural scientists and social scientists in regard to this question. Over two thirds of the natural scientists interviewed believed that it is possible to separate science from policy, whereas less than half of the interviewed social scientists felt this way.

More important, the comments of the interviewees provided insights into the reasons these beliefs exist. Natural scientists, for instance, tend to view science within the lens of the scientific method. That is, they tend to believe that if science is to mean anything worthwhile it must be protected from the value-laden world of politics. On the other hand, social scientists tend to believe that there is no such thing as neutral science that can somehow be separated from policy making. Science was viewed by the majority of interviewed social scientists as just one more ingredient in the policy (political) mix.

There does exist, however, a general consensus among all those interviewed (both natural scientists and social scientists) that scientists and policy makers function in two entirely different worlds and that neither scientists nor policy makers take the time to reach across this division for understanding. Policy makers were seen by the respondents as working in a world that requires quick and straight-forward answers, whereas scientists were seen as working in a world prone to long reaction times and complex solutions. One point emphasized by those interviewed was the lack of communication between scientists and policy makers. Some blamed policy makers for the lack of communication. Others blamed scientists. In addition, there exists a general view that if science is going to have any chance of providing meaningful input into the policy process, scientists are the ones who will have to make a better effort to interact and talk with policy makers. It was emphasized by many of those interviewed that scientists must do a much better job of translating their scientific findings into a format that is better understood by both policy makers and the public. The idea is that scientists must be more articulate and should refine their approach to policy makers in a way that would make policy makers pause to listen.

The final point that stood out from the interview results was how fervently many of the natural scientists felt about the way policy makers "shop" for science and scientists. An often mentioned belief among the interviewed natural scientists was that because much of the best science goes unheard by policy makers, who tend to listen only to the scientists that support their views, there exists a genuine frustration in the scientific community about the worth of science. There appears to be a feeling among those interviewed that politics is not only dominant but that the only science getting through to policy makers is the science that supports particular ideological views.

NOTES

1. Leiss stipulated that when he uses the term "science," he is referring to the natural sciences.

2. To review the scope and methods of these interviews, see Chapter 1.

3. These comments, as are all the other comments presented in this manner (for both Chapter 5 and Chapter 6), are gleaned from interviews the author conducted in 1997.

Chapter 6

Scientists, Advocacy, and Objectivity

LOST CREDIBILITY: SCIENTISTS AND ACID RAIN

One of the basic tenets of the scientific method is that scientists perform their research in an objective manner. As Bruce Bimber submitted: "The idealized image of the scientific expert involves not simply knowledge, but also a large element of objectivity, of being above politics and partisanship . . . [scientists] derive legitimacy from their ability to appeal to non-political professional standards" (1996, 12). However, as the preceding chapters have documented, one of the most dramatic (and troubling) charges that surfaced against United States scientists involved in acid rain research was that they blatantly disregarded the tenets of the scientific method (including objectivity) to lobby (advocate) for specific policy positions. It is a charge that goes way beyond the singular issue of acid rain. It goes straight to the heart of any discussion of how science is supposed to be linked to policy making.

In this regard, Daniel Sarewitz has maintained that in today's world of policy making there exists a persistent and sometimes vitriolic debate around the character and validity of the natural scientists and that this debate "hinges on the core assumption of science: that sometimes things are objectively knowable" (1996, ix). Furthermore, it is now posited that the very essence of science (its ability to produce objective results) is at risk because scientists are increasingly coming under immense pressure to provide more definitive answers than their current research can sustain (K.C. Cole and Hotz 1999, 4A). Some scholars now view this situation as one that has created "disturbing crises of integrity" for scientists (Zillman 1997, 1084).

Certainly, more and more scientists appear to be advocating for specific policy options. For instance, Patrick Hamlett has documented the move in recent years of scientists taking public positions on scientific and technological developments as proposed by government and industry. He observed that: "Because they enjoy considerable public prestige and trust, when scientists . . . decide to go public about a problem, they will be listened to and interviewed on television and will often mobilize public involvement in the issue at hand" (1992, 63). Helen Ingram, H. Brinton Milward, and Wendy Laird referred to a new form of science activism and networks of advocacy scientists, arguing that emerging environmental issues have led to a vast increase in the role of scientists as policy advocates (1990, 2–5). Ingram, Milward, and Laird also offered a critique of the idea that science activism is constrained by the rules of good science:

There has been concern that the close advisory role that scientists have come to play in government has meant that scientists too often lend their reputation for objectivity to legitimize positions and policies determined by government for reasons other than science. It may also be the case that the scientist's reputation for objectivity may be used to legitimize the special interests of some subfields or some scientific networks. In their zeal to obtain what they view as their fair share of attention, science advocates may exaggerate the significance of their findings. In the long run, such exaggeration may damage the overall status of the scientific community as well as distort the overall balance of effort directed to the many important science questions needing answers. (1990, 24–25)

Thus, the success of scientists in discovering environmental problems and offering solutions seems to have facilitated an increase in advocacy. Many argue that this advocacy has had a potent political impact. For example, Karen Litfin claimed that scientific opinion is valued because science and scientists serve as one of the primary sources of legitimation for environmental policy debates (1994, 9). Support for this point of view is provided by Lynton Caldwell, who proclaimed that science has been a major influence in changing attitudes toward the environment (1985, 222), and Marvin Soroos, who credited science with a substantial role in the creation and evolution of atmospheric environmental regimes (1997, 14).

The idea that scientists, especially those concerned with the environment, should leave the idealized world of detachment and objectivity to become full-fledged participants in the policy process appears to be gaining strength. This view has been supported by some who claim that scientists are the only ones with the knowledge and ability to translate the rapid deterioration of the global environment into terms that will prompt outrage from the general public and action from policy makers (Lubchenco 1998, 491–96; Myers and Reichert 1997, xix; Safina 1998, A80). In this same vein, others have cited the failure of scientists to educate Americans about the dangers of ecological destruction and have contended that scientists need to stop pretending to be above the political fray or they will be consigned to irrelevance in policy making (S. Meyer 1995, B1). In this regard, those who fear ecological destruction have argued that scientists have an obligation to inform public policy; an obligation to become political players in the environmental policy-making process.

But does this advocacy by scientists undermine the objectivity that many believe is the foundation for their influence in the policy process? How does such advocacy affect the legitimacy of science? These are crucial questions centering on the ability of scientists to provide reliable and ideologically neutral data to policy makers (Hamlett, 1992, 63). In attempting to answer these questions, Dorothy Nelkin claimed that scientists' power lies in their ability to be neutral arbiters of truth (1995, 453). She also contended that the willingness of scientists to lend their expertise to various factions in widely publicized disputes has undermined the assumptions about the objectivity of science (Nelkin 1995, 453). David Collingridge and Colin Reeve took this contention one step further by arguing that none of the myths supporting the traditional conception of science's special role in policy making can now be upheld; simply put, that science cannot deliver truth (1986, 28). Furthermore, Collingridge and Reeve see the role of scientists as neutral, disinterested, and detached observers as being ineffective. These authors have asserted that in order for scientists to be effective in the policy process, they must become active and interested parties; that is, scientists must act "more like advocates in a court of law than neutral scientists in the laboratory" (Collingridge and Reeve 1986, 17).

Regardless of advocacy, the question of whether objectivity is possible at all has been the focus of a long-running debate among philosophers of science. Many have argued that values are inherent and essential in both science and policy making (Finkel and Golding 1994, 69; Plutzer, Maney, and O'Connor 1998, 200–204). Nicholas Ashford submitted that it is an illusion to insist that values do not shape the choices that scientists make, from problem selection and data analysis to methodologies employed and the reporting of results (1995, 611). Walter Rosenbaum challenged what he calls the myth of socially neutral science because "it is now evident that many technical controversies in policy making may not be resolvable by resort to scientific evidence and argument, because 'scientific' solutions will be permeated with social, political, or economic bias. Indeed, political controversy often subverts scientific integrity. Experts can be readily, even unintentionally, caught up in the emotionally and politically polarizing atmosphere of such disputes, their judgment . . . badly compromised" (1998, 137).

Ingram, Milward, and Laird defined the rules of good science in terms of research being a collective effort in which scientists carefully build upon previously accumulated knowledge and where the research effort is based upon a scientist's ability to work independently, objectively, and accurately within a rigorous system of peer-review (1990, 8). However, these authors also claimed that the rules of good science are no longer sufficient to keep scientific research objective when faced with the pressures of advocacy (1990, 24–25).

Despite the attack on the tenets of the scientific process (especially on the concept of objectivity), it appears that the ideal of the independent, neutral scientist remains far from defunct. Scientist Ellis Cowling observed, "Objectivity is the hallmark of science and scholarship. It should not be given up lightly and especially not in return for a consulting fee!" (1988, 4). Echoing these sentiments, the journal *The Environmental Professional*, in an effort to directly address the trend toward advocacy science, recently published an issue dedicated to discussing a proposal to create a National Institute for the Environment. In this issue, many editors claimed that in today's climate of advocacy, science is disconnected from decision-makers and the public and scientific information is not credible (*The Environmental Professional* 1994, 117). The reason given for this dire situation, according to the editors of this journal, is that the United States suffers from the lack of an independent, nonpolitical, and respected source of environmental information.

Along this same line of thought, Megan Jones, David Guston, and Lewis Branscomb asserted that the most important characteristics of useful technical information and analysis pertain to the sources of the information rather than to the information itself (1996, 3). Moreover, they also maintained that these sources need to be trustworthy and accessible and that the most important attributes their work must exhibit are "accuracy, objectivity, and timeliness" (M. Jones, Guston, and Branscomb 1996, 3).

In a similar vein, Robert Proctor cautioned that while it is fashionable to claim that "all science is social," we should not forget that good reasons exist for scientists to distance their work from the questions of values and politics (1991, x). And while Sheila Jasanoff concluded that in both regulatory science and research science there can be no perfect, objectively verifiable truth, she also maintained that one can certainly hope for a serviceable truth, "a state of knowledge that satisfies tests of scientific acceptability and supports reasoned decisionmaking" (1990, 250). Furthermore, there are others within the scientific community who believe that objectivity can be approached in terms of degree, with the inherently interested process of advocacy at one end, and the ideal notion of disinterested expertise at the other (Bimber 1996, 14).

Essentially, the scholarly literature has described a policy world where there exist two major views of how the science-policy linkage operates. One view is that good science produces truth and that the truth-producers (i.e., scientists) deserve a special role in politics. According to this view, scientific knowledge is treated as a product that is generated by a process external to and quite different from the actual policy process. The policy process is perceived as treating scientific knowledge as objective and uninfluenced by political or social values (Williams and Matheny 1995, 53). As Litfin explained, many of the problems we face in relating science to policy are "rooted in the larger belief that science is objective and value-free, while political life is ideological and value-laden" (1994, 33).[1] This view also holds that satisfactory resolution of policy disputes is based on achieving scientific consensus, with emphasis on the ability of science and scientists to resolve uncertainty.

The second view is that scientific knowledge is a negotiated product of human inquiry, formed not by interactions among scientists alone but among scientists, research patrons, and regulatory adversaries (Cozzens and Woodhouse 1995, 534). According to this perspective, science is viewed as a social process that is "not immune from the values and biases of the wider society within which it is situated" (Williams and Matheny 1995, 53). In fact, this view of science decries the excessive and unrealistic expectations of science. It holds that politics reigns supreme and that science and scientists are merely ammunition in a larger political struggle over conflicting values, interests, and sources of power (Graham, Green, and Roberts 1988, 217–18). This view of science describes a world where scientists often become policy activists who advocate specific positions based on their belief systems and that these scientists are usually quite vocal in their participation (Wilkening 1997, 11).[2]

The first view, that good science produces truth, has come under tremendous fire in recent times. Bruce Bimber admitted that few serious observers of politics or science believe that facts and values can be clearly separated (1996, 4) and Leonard Cole pointed out that scientists who advocate contradictory positions cannot all be arguing "objective" science (1993, 7). These ideas have been supported by Adam Finkel and Dominic Golding, who have insisted that values are inherent in both science and the policy process (1994, 69), and by Jasanoff, who proclaimed the artificiality of maintaining a strict separation between science and politics (1990, 230).

In addition, the trend in environmental policy making appears to be moving away from the goal of achieving scientific consensus and toward a more adversarial use of science. In this regard, Mark Schaefer spoke of the increased use of "friendly facts," where parties to disputes come to the table with their own set of facts that are supposedly scientifically based (1998). At the same time, Daniel Sarewitz depicted a policy world where the absence of scientific consensus has led to the use of legitimate scientific experts to support the opposing sides of conflicts (1996, 76). The end result, according to Sarewitz, is that: "The capacity of scientific expertise to contribute to dispute resolution is therefore negated, and claims to authoritativeness must collapse, as political adversaries call upon highly credentialed and well-respected experts to bolster conflicting political positions" (1996, 76).

SCIENTISTS' PERCEPTIONS OF ADVOCACY AND OBJECTIVITY

Earlier chapters have described an acid rain debate that resulted in accusations that scientists (and science) did not deliver the truth. Critics decried the number of acid rain scientists who turned to policy advocacy in order to push both personal and political agendas. However, as described above, most scholars maintain that the expectation that scientists remain objective is just not realistic. It is now commonly accepted among those who study the science-policy linkage that science is inherently value-laden. Moreover, the scholarly literature reveals a policy world where advocacy by scientists is quite prevalent. In other words, it appears that more and more scientists have left the structured world of scientific inquiry and entered the chaotic world of policy advocacy.

It is time to turn again to the interviews with scientists to see how prevalent these views are among the scientific community. In this regard, the next two sections display the results of two questions asked of the 129 scientists interviewed for this study: "Should scientists advocate policy positions?" and "Is it possible for scientists to be objective in completing their research?"

Scientists and Advocacy

Interpretation of Table 6.1. The results of the interview question, "Should scientists advocate policy positions?" are presented in Table 6.1. An overwhelming percentage of both the natural scientists and social scientists interviewed for this study (73%; n=94) stated that scientists should advocate policy positions. This belief is consistent among both United States scientists and Canadian scientists as well as among natural scientists and social scientists. In fact, a good number of those scientists interviewed (19%; n=24) asserted not only that scientists should advocate, but that they have a moral responsibility to do so.[3]

Expressed several times (12%; n=16) was the thought that scientists should advocate because they are in the best position to make policy judgments, owing to their special knowledge. Another point made by some (9%; n=11) was that scientists must separate their duties as citizens from their duties as scientists. Respondents argued that as citizens, scientists have an obligation to speak out, but that as scientists they must maintain their professional indifference. In this regard, a point that was made again and again is that scientists must always state when they are speaking as citizens and when they are speaking as scientists. Finally, a number of respondents (12%; n=16) spoke of the severe consequences for scientists who do advocate. There exists a concern among those interviewed that when scientists do advocate policy positions, they put themselves immediately at risk of losing their professional credibility within the scientific community.

What Respondents Said. Those respondents who saw advocacy as a moral responsibility used such phrases as a scientist's "duty to carry the science forward" and responsibility to "spread the word." A Canadian natural scientist put it in these terms:

No person is just a scientist. We have a social and moral responsibility to speak out more than just describing. But we must do so openly and modestly, recognizing the possibility of error.

Another Canadian natural scientist stated his views in no uncertain terms.

I have always argued that scientists not only be allowed to advocate but have the responsibility to articulate their work, to describe what kinds of policy responses should result from their work. Scientists should have that right. Most do not. Scientists must be thinking about the "so what" of their work and use whatever routes available to do it, to get the word out.

Table 6.1
Scientists' Perceptions of Advocacy

The interview question was: "Should scientists advocate policy positions?"

PART A: Number of answers given by category (as coded by author)

	United States		Canada	
	Natural Scientists (n=33)	Social Scientists (n=32)	Natural Scientists (n=33)	Social Scientists (n=31)
Yes	21	24	23	26
No	12	8	10	5

PART B: Comments (by number of times cited)

	United States		Canada	
	Natural Scientists (n=33)	Social Scientists (n=32)	Natural Scientists (n=33)	Social Scientists (n=31)
Scientists have a moral responsibility to advocate	2	5	8	9
Scientists lose credibility if they advocate	2	7	4	3
Scientists should advocate because they have special knowledge	5	1	7	3
Scientists have a right to advocate because they are citizens in a democracy	7	3	4	2
Scientists can advocate if they make clear they are acting as citizens and not scientists	3	5	1	2

Source: Author's Computation.

Respondents spoke of times "when the issue and evidence is so clear" that scientists would be "irresponsible" and "guilty" if they did not speak out. A United States natural scientist described the quandary many scientists often find themselves in with respect to this obligation to pursue the moral high ground.

It is pretty risky to try to do both science and advocacy. On the other hand, there are issues where if scientists were not advocating, no one else would be. Global climate change is one such issue. It was scientists who initially sounded the alarm. It was effects documented by scientists investigating and able to identify and demonstrate [that a problem existed]. And if scientists weren't doing it, nobody else would.

These moral and social responsibilities were considered obligations by many respondents because of a scientist's special knowledge. However, many of the interviewed social scientists stated that they did not believe scientists should receive any special considerations when it comes to commenting on policy issues.

Scientists aren't especially any better off than others in making policy choices and I'm sometimes impressed with how naive scientists are when they get into the policy field.

Natural scientists are equipped to tell you about the natural processes but are not equipped to inform on policies. For that you need to have a clear understanding of cost-benefit analyses. But natural scientists don't have that expertise.

Scientists are citizens and have obligations. On the other hand, it can be very difficult because sometimes the public takes them as experts beyond their particular expertise. Scientists should not be given special weight in some circumstances. It is amazing to me the arrogance of some of these so-called experts, like their word should be counted as the same as ten people.

Scientists do not have the credentials to make policy judgments. As soon as you do that you are no longer a scientist, and I am not sure all scientists understand that distinction.

Scientists must be cautious because they don't know enough about the unintended consequences of their policy initiatives or of the subtleties of using economic and social points as tools. They end up stepping past their scientific capabilities.

In contrast, the interviewed natural scientists were more apt to believe that scientists are in a better position than any other citizens to participate in policy making.

Some scientists are truly enlightened and have a point of view they believe. If they are experts in the field, they should stand up and be heard.

The traditional view is that scientists are there as cogs in the wheel to provide the technical information and interpretation that can be taken by those who see the whole picture and put it in the box with everything else and come to a decision at a far higher level than mere mortals can. Everyone says that. It is the standard answer at testimonies and in the public. But I think there is room for a counter argument under the assumption that if we understand our own results better than any outsiders can or do and if it points to a certain policy position then it is OK to say that. Now that might not be the same thing as advocating but no conversation is neutral.

If scientists have information important for policy they should definitely state their opinion. Scientists should be more actively involved than they have been, especially in the environmental arena. Scientists should get involved with policy-relevant research and not just do research to do research.

Many natural scientists also felt that it was very important that scientists living in a democratic society must separate their role as scientists from their role as citizens.

Scientists must be able to separate personal and professional behavior, one as citizen and one as scientist. If making a speech to the Sierra Club, I say right up front and want the press to understand that I'm acting as a citizen and not as a member of [my university]. But when it comes to my data, I can be as much [of] a damn advocate as I please and that's my right and responsibility.

Yes, scientists should advocate, with qualifications. I do this frequently, where I say this is what I have to say about the science and then take my hat off as a scientist and put my hat on as a citizen. And I would even go further and say that it would be shirking one's duty not to do that, to "not say" what ought to be done.

The role of an individual environmental scientist is to be objective and do objective analysis of the environment, to do basic science only, to determine how nature works. If you start being an advocate then you must take the scientist's hat off and be clear you are doing it only as a citizen.

Another natural scientist explained advocacy in terms of frustration and need.

Occasionally you get so frustrated by the lack of action that you do go public to advocate. You become very frustrated with the inability of the sheer weight of the evidence to produce any action. Sometimes there comes a time in your best judgment that the ends justify the means. But this also pushes the science beyond credibility. We're all guilty from time to time.

Yet, many natural scientists were adamant that scientists should not advocate under any circumstances, that the loss of credibility within their profession is just too great a risk.

If we are going to become party to causes, then that's what we become, party to causes. We lose our scientific credentials when we become party to causes. If we want respect as scientific specialists [we cannot confuse] what scientists know about the facts and what they think society should do about the facts. It took me a long time to learn this lesson. But from my congressional experience, when a congressman asked "What should we do?" I should have had the good sense to say "You are the decision maker and I am the scientist and let's not confuse the two."

Scientists are not advocates and they shouldn't be. If they go too far, their reputations will be messed up. I am an ecologist, a scientist. But people sometimes think because of that that I'm an environmentalist, that they are the same thing. Now I may have environmental leanings, but in my profession as an ecologist I follow the scientific method. As a professional I do the science dispassionately. Environmentalists follow emotional paths as advocates and there is a big difference.

The job of scientists is to find out what nature is trying to tell us and that's different from the notion of what we want to happen. That taints the analysis and breaks objectivity. Objective science is practiced less and less. There are many more advocates and advocates have no credibility in my view. I don't believe a thing they say.

In the end, though, the vast majority of both natural and social scientists from the United States and Canada felt that despite the drawbacks, scientists should (and must) advocate policy positions. As a Canadian social scientist put it:

Scientists can advocate as long as they don't become advocates. You have individual scientists who end up being extremely powerful spokespeople because as scientists they have one foot in the pond of objectivity. So long as all scientists don't become radical "so-and-so's," then some legitimacy still remains. If they all go, then no objectivity is left.

Scientists and Objectivity

Interpretation of Table 6.2. The results of the second interview question, "Is it possible for scientists to be objective?" are presented in Table 6.2. [The word "objective" was not defined for those being interviewed. It was left up to each individual respondent to answer the question based on his or her interpretation of what objective meant.] The same differences found between natural scientists and social scientists with respect to their views of the separation of science from policy (see Chapter 5) were present in the responses to this question on objectivity: A much higher percentage of natural scientists (67%;n=44) than social scientists (43%; n=19) asserted that it is possible for scientists to be objective in completing their research. In addition, there was essentially no substantial difference between United States and Canadian scientists in their responses to this question.

Two other interesting points stand out from the interviews. First, a tangible percentage of those interviewed (22%; n=29), while denying the possibility that individual scientists could be objective, did espouse the idea that the scientific *process* provides a means of objectivity. Further, this finding is consistent among both natural scientists and social scientists. This faith that the scientific process filters out bias is important to note because when those who have enough faith in the scientific process (to be objective) are combined with those who have faith in the ability of individual scientists (to complete their research objectively), 71 percent (n=92) of all those interviewed argued that scientific objectivity is a realistic goal. This finding is completely contrary to the vast majority of the scholarly literature written on the science-policy linkage (as

Table 6.2
Scientists' Perceptions of Objectivity

The interview question was: "Is it possible for scientists to be objective?"

PART A: Number of answers given by category (as coded by author)

	United States		Canada	
	Natural Scientists (n=33)	**Social Scientists (n=32)**	**Natural Scientists (n=33)**	**Social Scientists (n=31)**
Yes	20	7	24	12
No	6	13	4	14
Individual scientists cannot be objective; but scientific process provides a means to objectivity	7	12	5	5

PART B: Comments (by number of times cited)

	United States		Canada	
	Natural Scientists (n=33)	**Social Scientists (n=32)**	**Natural Scientists (n=33)**	**Social Scientists (n=31)**
Science is subsumed by societal/cultural values	4	9	4	8

Source: Author's Computation.

highlighted earlier), which claims that the idea of science being value-free has been clearly (and finally) debunked. At least among those interviewed for this study, it appears that the idea of objectivity is still very much alive within the scientific community.

Second, despite the large percentage of respondents that retain their faith in objectivity, there exists a recognition among many of the respondents (19%; n=25) that science is subsumed by societal and cultural values. However, it is also important to understand that many more social scientists (by a 2-to-1 margin) mentioned this point than did natural scientists.

What Respondents Said. Natural scientists tended to defend objectivity as one of the essential qualities of being a scientist. One natural scientist stated that he would have a "hard time being a scientist if [he] didn't believe [he] could be objective" and another stated that scientists would "not be true to their scientific credentials" and would be "abusing science" if they did not regularly practice objectivity. Other natural scientists spoke of objectivity as the "measure of their worth as a scientist" and argued that "if scientists are not being objective, then they are being dishonest." This point of view is summed up by two different natural scientists (the first from Canada and the second from the United States):

Yes, scientists can be objective. In fact, that is exactly what makes for the integrity of science and scientists and separates them from others. It is extremely important to be just and true and science has to be seen as being that, having integrity of scientific thought and judgment.

It is impossible to be objective. As human beings, it is probably not unusual for people to have a tendency to be affected by their subjective beliefs. But good scientists recognize that they would be compromising their science and would avoid that.

One natural scientist decried what he viewed as a recent trend to abandon objectivity as a goal of scientists.

What worries me is that we have even abandoned objectivity as a goal. Scientists ought to struggle for objectivity and show disdain for advocacy. But neither the public nor the administration shares this belief of mine. You get research dollars if you choose the side that they want to hear.

A large portion of the interviewed social scientists, on the other hand, were not sure "there is anything like objectivity because the way we see the world colors all we do" and observed that many scientists "mislead themselves because they don't realize that science is just one of the many cultural activities that inform policy." Along these lines, a Canadian social scientist stated that "the only person who is capable of being objective would be institutionalized as insane because objectivity requires detachment and they are the only people who are truly detached." A United States social scientist argued that we needed to distinguish between objectivity and honesty.

It is possible for scientists to be honest, but honesty is not the same as objective. There are three different concepts: honesty, objectivity, and balance. Objectivity equals looking at all the evidence without psychological (or other) influences which would cause the interpretation or conclusions to be spun and that is near nigh impossible for anybody to [do]. Objectivity can be more or less true and is an ideal that is never achievable. One can be balanced in the sense that you include minority interpretations and literature on the other side, the contrary viewpoints, and provide a fair description and fair space for these. And you can be quite honest about what you know and do not know. Science began with this view but now science is tremendously corrupted by the sins of omission, just leaving it all out. People decide to leave out or short-shift the contrary points of view. Scientists are not honest when they leave these out. You have to acknowledge the contrary data. But I believe very few scientists do that today.

And a United States natural scientist described how forces on the policy-making side of the equation were slowly but surely compromising his professional objectivity.

We like to think we are being truly objective, but in fact we are not. Now the numbers are never fudged, but slowly but surely the scope, the audience, and the questions we are asking are being shaped by what we think EPA finds interesting. I will stand completely behind the science, but the process is not efficient. We keep rewriting the budgets and grants to fit what EPA wants. So it is easy to see that the science is biased in substance, like in the questions being addressed. We are very objective as far as our work is concerned. But we would have done things differently if resources and money were just given to us as scientists to do the work. But EPA is responding to a different master, the policy makers, and we scientists have been jerked around for many years.

Of special note are the number of respondents, both natural scientists and social scientists, who felt that it did not matter whether individual scientists could be objective because the scientific process was designed to deal with this contingency. That is:

There is this notion of inter-subjectivity where it is not so much that individual scientists are objective but that as a group they will come to some finding that is possible.

It is not always easy to be objective, particularly when in a politically charged arena. But we have the scientific process that is self-correcting, a process driven by empirical data as objective as humanly possible. This equals the scientific process and it is the ideal we should all strive for. But everyone is human and we never fully live up to those ideals. But that is why we have a self-correcting process and where replication takes over. Science is an intensely human endeavor full of mistakes. But by nature it is the best process as opposed to all the other processes. It gets you on the right track. Sooner or later it will come down to the right answer. My fear is that we do not let the process run its course.

There is a difference between science (the process) and scientists (the people). Scientists are people driven by personal interest and career. They want numbers to come out and I do not trust scientists. But it is reasonably satisfactory to trust science. Science provides checks and balances. I trust science, not the individual scientist.

Scientists do not need to be objective. The point is inter-subjective consistency; that's what replication is designed for. The process allows lots of other people to look at what you are doing and in the end it will all come out. The process will weed it all out.

Can scientists be objective? That is the wrong question. It is not objectivity, but replicability. The definition of science isn't what you believe or don't believe, it is a question of replication. It would be a cruel burden to ask an individual scientist to be objective. Scientists are not objective in the least. Objectivity is irrelevant and so is passion. What counts is whether someone else can do it.

SUMMARY OF INTERVIEW FINDINGS

The vast majority of scientists interviewed for this study expressed the view that scientists should advocate for specific policy proposals. This was true for both natural and social scientists and for both United States and Canadian scientists. Furthermore, those interviewed spoke of scientists' special knowledge and their moral responsibility to disseminate that knowledge in a public forum. Respondents also argued that scientists had the right (and obligation) to participate in policy debates *as citizens* as long as they made it perfectly clear to their audience which hat they were wearing. There were also a good number of respondents who argued that advocacy by scientists went hand-in-hand with the loss of a scientist's credibility within the scientific community.

The overall figures from the tables also show that the way Canadian scientists and United States scientists view the concept of objectivity is quite similar. However, the results do indicate a substantial difference in the way natural scientists and social scientists view the concept of objectivity. A much larger percentage of natural scientists than social scientists tended to express the opinion that it was possible for individual scientists to complete their research objectively. Also, a much larger number of social scientists than natural scientists mentioned the fact that science is greatly affected by societal and cultural values. On the other hand, many of those interviewed (both natural scientists and social scientists) observed that the scientific process could filter out the biases of individual scientists.

NOTES

1. Litfin also points out that while this view is faulty because facts are socially constructed, it is nevertheless influential (1994, 33).

2. Kenneth Wilkening distinguishes between three categories of individual scientists: the policy inactive, the policy active, and the policy activists (1997, 11). The policy inactive are those who produce policy-relevant scientific information but are not involved in the policy process. The policy active are those who not only produce scientific knowledge but also participate in the policy process (e.g., they may sit on policy-oriented advisory committees). The policy activists advocate a specific policy position based on a belief system and are usually quite vocal in their participation.

3. It should be noted that the belief in a scientist's moral and social obligation to advocate is more prevalent among Canadian than United States respondents.

Chapter 7

Acid Rain: From Science to Policy

THE POLICY PROCESS

This book began with the purpose of providing a description and analysis of the science-policy linkage that defined the policy debate over acid rain in the United States. To accomplish this task, the evolution of the United States policy dealing with acid rain was viewed through the lens of John Kingdon's model of the policy-making process. Within this context, acid rain was recognized as an area of concern and determined to be worthy of government action. It was called "the most important and controversial environmental problem of the decade" (Gould 1985, 4) and "one of the more prominent, complex, and divisive policy issues of the 1980s" (Ihara 1985, 3). Priority was given to finding a solution to the acid rain problem and hundreds of millions of dollars were allocated to determine possible alternatives for abatement. While no crisis or focusing event was forthcoming to push acid rain to the forefront of the decision-making process, it remained a salient issue to policy makers for an extended period of time.

In the end, the decision to reduce acid rain pollutants in the United States by approximately 50 percent (from the 1980 levels) followed the recommendation of the very first major scientific report on acid rain, which was released by the National Academy of Sciences in the early 1980s. Yet, it took nearly 10 years of very contentious political debate for policy makers in the United States to finally agree with that recommendation. Why did it take policy makers so long to make that substantive decision?

One of the reasons why policy stalemate occurred was the ability of those opposed to acid rain controls to frame the debate in terms that supported a cautious approach to acting on reducing pollution. For instance, those opposed to controls were able to portray the costs of controls as certain and high, coming in the form of higher taxes, job losses, higher electric bills, and even possible lifestyle changes. Opponents of controls were also able to frame the debate by attacking the science put forth by the Canadians, who staunchly supported controls. John Dingell, a powerful member of the United States Congress, was particularly effective in focusing the debate on questions about foreign interference in a strictly United States domestic decision-making process and on questions about the credibility of the science. He and others opposed to acid rain controls were able to portray the issue as one filled with scientific uncertainty: uncertainty about the extent of the present and future damage, uncertainty about whether reductions in the precursors of acid rain would really solve the problem (or even drastically reduce the pollution from acid rain), and uncertainty about the best time to begin controls.

CRITICISM OF THE SCIENCE-POLICY LINKAGE

The scientific uncertainty surrounding the acid rain issue became one of the key factors in the policy makers' ability to defer making a decision about establishing controls to reduce pollution levels. Despite the efforts of some of the most highly respected scientists in the acid rain field of study, the adequacy and credibility of the scientific findings were continually questioned. At no time during the debate did policy makers, as a whole, accept the idea that scientific consensus existed on either the causes or effects of acid rain. The final acid rain policy established by the United States came about slowly and, according to most observers, the science (and scientists) played an important, but questionable, role.

On the positive side, Don Munton asserted that over time the common perception and dominant discourse about acid rain changed substantially and that science was an important ingredient of this change. In this regard, Munton maintained that the gradual and continual accumulation of scientific research made it increasingly untenable for United States policy makers to argue against the need for acid rain controls (1997b, 23). This view, that the persistent and cumulative effort of scientists contributed substantially to the drive toward an acid rain policy, was supported by many scientists who participated in the policy-making process (see Lackey and Blair 1997, 9–10; Schindler 1992, 124).

However, there are also those who downplayed the importance of the role that science played in the ultimate decision to reduce acid rain pollutants and even suggested that one of the casualties of the acid rain debate was scientific credibility (see Loucks 1993, 71–72; Perhac 1991a, 38–40; Roberts 1991, 1302; Rubin, Lave, and Morgan 1991–92, 47–48). In this context, three general criticisms of the science-policy linkage were made. The first is that scientists wield very little influence on policy makers. In the acid rain debate this is illustrated by two things: (1) Nearly all of the major scientific reports of the early 1980s by well-established and well-respected scientific entities recommended reduction in acid rain pollutants. Yet, no action was taken to reduce these pollutants for nearly a decade; and (2) The final NAPAP report, which was supposed to provide guidance for the ultimate acid rain policy decision, was not released in its final form to policy makers until after an acid rain policy was already in place.

Second, because scientists and policy makers operate in two different worlds under different sets of rules, science and policy will seldom converge. Policy makers work under severe time constraints, have to make almost instantaneous decisions, and are accountable to the values and ideologies that define their professional existence. Scientists, on the other hand, work under constant uncertainty and have a perspective that is defined over an extended period of time. Further, scientists are bound by the scientific process, which, according to its basic tenets, is supposed to be void of values and ideologies. In the case of acid rain this tension is illustrated by the numerous and continual clashes between scientists and policy makers at the congressional hearings on acid rain.

The third criticism is that science is corrupted by politics. Instead of providing objective advice and counsel to policy makers, scientists are viewed as becoming advocates for particular policy proposals. In essence, scientists become purveyors of established values and ideologies instead of providing good science. This is illustrated in the acid rain debate in two ways: (1) Many of the scientists who testified at the congressional hearings were paid consultants of the electrical power industry (including coal interests) or of established environmental groups, both of which had clearly established policy goals built around their self-interests; and (2) Many of the scientists who testified at the congressional hearings on acid rain offered their personal opinions as well as their scientific findings.

SCIENTISTS RESPOND TO CRITICISM

In light of these criticisms of the science-policy linkage, several of our most eminent scientists have outlined what they believe are the lessons to be learned from the acid rain experience about the interface between science and public policy. Milton Russell, the former chairman of the NAPAP Oversight Review Board, submitted that the acid rain experience reinforced several basic principles regarding linking science to policy (1992, 110). First, the proper role of science should be to advise on what is practicably achievable, not to seek to influence what the policy questions should be. Second, the scientific community should strictly adhere to the canons of the scientific process, including peer review. Third, a clear need exists for a series of highly selective, semipermeable barriers between scientists and policy makers that filter the influence of each. In this regard, Russell believes that scientists doing and reporting their research must be protected from the undue influence of policy makers concerning what they find and report, and that policy makers must be protected from scientists telling them what they should decide.

Ellis Cowling, one of the scientists credited with bringing NAPAP into being, asserted that science and technology alone cannot ever hope to provide the wisdom to make enlightened choices; that is, wisdom derives not only from science but also from the humanities. Cowling declared that the responsibility of scientists in a democracy is to understand and clearly communicate the scientific facts and uncertainties and to describe expected outcomes objectively (1992, 113–14). He further argued that deciding what to do involves questions of societal values and that scientists have no special authority to make those decisions. Cowling also insisted that careful and precise communications are needed among all parties in the decision-making processes; among scientists, policy analysts, and decision makers themselves, between each of these groups, and between each of these groups and the public at large. In addition, Cowling spoke very frankly about how he views advocacy by scientists. "Objectivity and the willingness to consider new scientific or scholarly evidence on its merit are among the few things that distinguish scientists . . . from lay-persons in our society. For this reason, scientists who become advocates for social or political causes do so at some peril of losing both their objectivity and their credibility" (1988, 8).

Robert Lackey [associate director for science] and Roger Blair [chief of the regional branch of the Western Ecology Division] of the National Health and Environmental Effects Research Laboratory of the Environmental Protection Agency in Corvalis, Oregon, set forth what they believe are the lessons learned for scientists from the acid rain experience (1997, 11–12). They called for scientists to beware of political efforts to use their scientific enterprise to focus on questions that tend to support a particular political position. They also warn scientists to ignore the siren call to substitute personal values for scientific independence. Lackey and Blair believe that moving from the scientific "is" to the policy "ought" under the guise of sound science is only a small step. Furthermore, they warned that such behavior may cause a loss of credibility among colleagues that will be remembered long after Congress and the public have moved on to other issues.

These same sentiments are reflected in comments from another group of scientists (including Robert Lackey) who recently published a critique of science and policy as it applied to acid rain research. Derek Winstanley [chief of the Illinois State Water Survey and former director of NAPAP], Lackey, Walter Warnick [director of the Office of Scientific and Technical Information for the Department of Energy], and John Malanchuk [vice president for Air Quality and Multi-Media Compliance of the International Technology Corporation and former deputy director of NAPAP] insisted that the most important task for scientists is to ensure that the integrity of the scientific process is upheld. In this regard, Winstanley et al. claimed that when scientists interject their personal values into their findings, they necessarily compromise their scientific objectivity and that "[w]hile scientists are also members of a democratic society and have every right to recommend political actions, it is inevitable that the audience will not be able to separate their technical and nontechnical conclusions. The challenge is to stimulate open scientific investigation and reporting and to separate these from advocacy" (1998, 55).

Finally, Ralph Perhac, the former director of the Environmental Science Department for the Electric Power Research Institute and a key figure in acid rain research, also offered several recommendations for making science (and scientists) more useful to policy makers (1991a, 38–40; 1991b, 26–49). First, Perhac suggested that if science is to be trusted and have an impact on the national scene, scientists must make a concerted effort to separate fact from policy judgment. Second, he argued that science must be demonstrably credible and based on rigorous peer review and clear identification of nonscientific opinion. Third, Perhac believes that more emphasis should be placed on policy-related research (i.e., studies to answer questions facing decision makers) instead of research done merely to obtain the best scientific information.

The points of convergence of the scientists cited above are clear and unambiguous. They believe that no matter what the cost, scientists must adhere to the canons of the scientific process. This process, including the ideal of objectivity, is what distinguishes and separates scientists from all other interested parties. In this regard, scientists are not to advocate social or political causes at any time. If scientists do turn to advocacy, they will lose the very things that make them special: their objectivity and their credibility. Furthermore, to help ensure that scientists can remain true to their scientific principles, scientists and policy makers must be separated in such a manner that protects each from the vagaries of the other. In other words, scientists and policy makers must be separated by a semipermeable barrier that protects each from the influence of the other (Russell 1992, 108).

PERCEPTIONS OF SCIENTISTS

When one looks carefully at the ideas put forth by some of North America's most highly regarded natural scientists (as delineated above), it is not difficult to see that they directly address some of the concerns and criticisms that plagued scientists during the decade-long policy debate over acid rain. Furthermore, these commentators (among others) basically suggested that scientists must remain committed to the tenets of the scientific process. Scientists were asked to clearly communicate the scientific facts to policy makers in an objective manner and to refrain from any type of policy advocacy. But is this possible? Much of the recent scholarly literature (as reviewed earlier) suggests that it is not possible. Yet, some of the most respected scientists involved in acid rain research remain convinced that it is not only possible, but necessary if scientists are to retain their unique position of credibility within the policy-making process.

The views of the scientists cited above should not be taken lightly. They represent the thoughts and considerations of scientists renowned within the scientific community for their scientific expertise. Moreover, they represent the ideas of scientists who have had substantial experience with respect to acid rain, especially as it pertains to NAPAP. That having been said, it must also be recognized that these are the views of only a few select scientists who felt it necessary to speak out and took the time to publicize their recommendations throughout the scientific community and beyond. While important, these views may not necessarily represent the vast majority of scientists involved with acid rain research. That is where the interview results come into play.

Advocacy, Objectivity, and the Separation of Science and Policy: The Interviews

The interview results represent a sampling of both natural and social scientists and of United States and Canadian scientists. The views of the 129 scientists interviewed for this study added a richness to the views of the select few quoted above. Moreover, the views of the interviewed scientists suggested that there exist several different levels of commitment to the canons of the scientific process within the scientific community as a whole.

It is important to recognize that a majority of the interviewed scientists thought that policy makers do listen to scientists. However, few of those interviewed believed that science has a strong influence on policy makers. In fact, the majority of both natural and social scientists interviewed for this study perceive that the relationship between scientists and policy makers is skewed toward the policy (and political) side, with policy makers having the ability to manipulate, ignore, and frame science as they see fit. In this light, many of those interviewed stated that one of the primary reasons policy makers do not listen to scientists is because scientists do not consistently communicate the science to policy makers in a meaningful manner. That is, the respondents sensed that at times the science is not getting through and that scientists must do a better job of packaging their findings in a way that is more understandable and appealing to policy makers.

The gap perceived to exist between scientists and policy makers is important, because it appears that these two groups do not speak in the same language and that neither group has taken the time to learn the intricacies of the other's profession and training. According to those interviewed, policy makers continue to ask scientists for "yes or no" and "right or wrong" answers, somehow expecting scientists to produce results in that format. And scientists keep hedging their findings in probabilities that often appear incomprehensible (and unusable) to policy makers. A strong contingent of natural scientists whole-heartedly criticized policy makers for their arrogance and ignorance. Many of the natural scientists held policy makers in low esteem and asserted that they are incapable of ever understanding what science is about.

More surprising, though, was the number of natural scientists who put the blame squarely on themselves. In other words, many natural scientists argued that the burden of resolving the problems that exist between scientists and policy makers lies with scientists. It is the scientists, they felt, who must make the effort to translate the complexities of science into a language that is understandable to both policy makers and the public at large. As stated earlier, many of the interviewed scientists perceived that it is all in the "packaging" of what scientists have to say. What this means in practical terms is that some scientists believe that those within the scientific community are going to have to change. They have come to the realization that if the good science is going to get through, scientists (not the policy makers) are going to have to work much harder in order to make their work more accessible and understandable. There was no doubt (at least among those interviewed) that the burden is squarely on the scientists to make this work.

In support of what Russell, Cowling, and the other scientists cited above have contended, the interviews revealed that a large number of natural scientists remain committed to the belief that it is possible for scientists to be objective in completing their research and to separate science from policy making. Despite the repeated pronouncements in the scholarly literature to the contrary, many natural scientists continue to cling to the beliefs that the scientific component of decision making can be separated from the political component and that scientists can provide ideologically neutral data to policy makers.

Furthermore, a large percentage of the natural scientists interviewed were adamant that it is their objectivity that defines who and what they are. Time after time, natural scientists contended that it is their ability to be objective that separates scientists from all other interested parties and provides them with special status within the policy-making process. And they argued that if an individual scientist occasionally strays from objective leanings, the scientific process is always present to make sure the end results remain true and correct. Simply put, many natural scientists expressed the view that replication provides insurance that science, in the end, will produce the truth.

At the same time, contrary to the views of Russell, Cowling, and others, a large majority of natural scientists and social scientists interviewed for this study overwhelmingly agreed that scientists should advocate policy positions. While this may seem odd (given the fact that a majority of the natural scientists interviewed also attached great importance to scientific objectivity and to the need for separating science and policy), this finding should be viewed in the context of what Walter Rosenbaum has described as the treacherous zone between science and politics that compels public officials to make scientific pronouncements and scientists to resolve policy issues, when neither is trained to make such judgments (1998, 126). Basically, the interviewed natural scientists saw themselves as attempting to function in two different worlds under two different sets of rules. On the one hand, they felt strongly about the need to retain their scientific objectivity; indeed, they believe it is following this tenet of the scientific method that separates scientists from all other interested parties. On the other hand, they also felt they have a moral and civic responsibility to ensure that the good science is getting into the policy debate.

This belief appears to tie in directly with the understanding natural scientists have that the burden of effective communications with policy makers lies with scientists. If policy makers are having difficulty understanding the science or connecting the science to the policy world, then scientists have a duty to make that connection in a way that is universally understood. Of course, putting the science into policy-relevant terms means that scientists can easily cross the line from scientist to advocate. Scientists can become so frustrated with the misuse (or nonuse) of their scientific findings that they feel compelled to join the policy debate so that the importance (in their view) of their findings is made perfectly clear. In brief, there is a belief among many of the natural scientists interviewed that there comes a time when the science must be put in its proper perspective and that those in the best position to do so are the natural scientists themselves.

Many of the interviewed natural scientists maintained that they could balance both worlds. In other words, they expressed the belief that it is possible to separate personal and professional behavior under the guise of acting as citizens at one time and acting as scientists at other times. This view, about the linkage of science to politics in a democracy such as the United States or Canada, is bolstered by the belief among those scientists interviewed that if they continue to work within the confines of the scientific process (with its systematic use of peer review and replication), all values will eventually be filtered out. Time after time, the natural scientists interviewed for this study professed their complete confidence in their ability to separate their role as scientists from their role as citizens. There was no doubt in the minds of many of the natural scientists interviewed that, as long as they openly and publicly announced when they were speaking as a scientist and when they were speaking as a citizen, they were not advocating under the guise of the scientific method, but were acting as any other interested citizen might in a democratic society.

But the idea that one can simply take off the scientific hat and put on the citizen hat at one's convenience is the very thing that brought on the wrath (and criticism) of scientists like Loucks, Perhac, and Schindler. It is also one of the things that appears to separate the perceptions of natural scientists from those of social scientists. On the whole, the interviewed social scientists were not of the view that scientists are capable of separating scientific work from policy outcomes. Nor are social scientists convinced (as many natural scientists appear to be) that scientists can complete their research in a completely objective manner.

One of the things that both natural scientists and social scientists appear to agree upon, however, is that by venturing into the policy arena, scientists risk losing their standing in the scientific community. Yet, according to the interview responses in this research project, more and more scientists are willing to take that chance. They believe that if policy makers are choosing which science to use based on their ideological bent rather than on an evaluation of the science itself, then scientists have a civic duty to communicate their views (i.e., advocate) in the context of what they, as both scientists and citizens, believe is important. Essentially, many scientists have decided that policy makers should not be left alone to frame scientific knowledge according to their political needs and that scientists have a responsibility and obligation to ensure that policy decisions are indeed based on good science (meaning science explained and communicated by the scientists themselves).

The United States–Canada Dichotomy

It is important to note that, except for a few instances, there were no substantial differences between United States and Canadian respondents with respect to the four interview questions asked. Slightly higher percentages of Canadian respondents were apt to believe that scientists could be objective in completing their research and to believe that scientists should advocate policy positions. This similarity of response allowed a more meaningful focus on the substance of the questions that were asked.

Moreover, this is an important finding because of the asymmetry in the United States–Canadian environmental sphere, especially as it pertains to acid rain (as described in the introductory chapter). There exists a clear imbalance with respect to the cross-border environmental relationship (with Canada often described as environmentally dependent on the United States) and with respect to acid rain (with Canada receiving the bulk of the pollution). However, the fact that scientists on both sides of the border share similar views about the role of science and scientists in the environmental policy-making process is quite significant. Despite the immense differences in the way these two countries approached the acid rain issue and the very contentious nature of the acid rain debate between Canada and the United States, it appears that scientists remain more closely bound by their scientific and professional ethics than by their nationalities.

This is an important finding, for several reasons. First, it provides evidence that the different national contexts of these scientists may not be the driving force determining their outlook and assessments. In essence, the lack of substantial differences between the perceptions of United States and Canadian scientists offers evidence of the separation of the worlds of science and politics, and shows that the institutions of science may be stronger and more independent of social and political concerns than they are generally given credit for in today's world. It also provides important evidence to support the natural scientists' contention that they can indeed do research that is relatively objective and value-free.

Furthermore, the natural-social science differences of opinion on advocacy and objectivity suggest that, in fact, the important distinction is not a national one, but a disciplinary one. It may be that the institutions of natural science are strong and independent enough from society that the focus of study should be more on why the perceptions of social scientists are so different from the perceptions of natural scientists. It may also be that social science institutions are highly penetrated by social, national, or governmental values already, and that this is why they can speak more clearly to policy makers and get into less trouble within their own social scientific communities for their advocacy practices.

The fact that United States and Canadian scientists line up so closely on their perceptions of the science-policy linkage is a positive sign of things to come. This is important, because there remains much work to be accomplished with respect to the acid rain issue. In fact, the recent release of the *Continental Pollutant Pathways* report by the Commission for Environmental Cooperation (CEC) makes it very clear that transboundary pollution continues to threaten human health and natural resources and that its reduction is not possible without cross-border attention and cooperation: "Acting alone, no nation of North America will be able to protect adequately its domestic environment or its citizens from pollutants transported along continental pathways. While pollutants are not constrained by political boundaries, programs to reduce them often are, and domestic decisions continue to be made with little reference to their implication for all of North America" (Lichtinger 1997, vii).[1] The hope that cross-border pollution can be reduced to the satisfaction of all countries involved remains strong, due both to the past record of United States–Canadian cooperation with respect to the environmental concerns of each country and, I would argue, to the fact that scientists in both countries share similar perceptions about the role of science in the environmental policy-making process.

The Natural-Social Science Dichotomy

The interview results of this study also indicate that scientists continue to struggle with their relationship to policy makers and that real differences remain between how natural scientists and social scientists perceive the science-policy linkage. Understanding these differences is helpful in evaluating the part that science plays in the environmental policy-making process. One key to that understanding lies in the movement toward advocacy by scientists. Along these lines, it is important to remember that a consensus of the scientists interviewed thought policy makers do listen. In this regard, the interview results identify a broad consensus, crossing disciplines, in favor of advocacy by scientists. But I would argue that one's view on advocacy depends on one's view of the relationship of advocacy to objectivity.

In short, the interview results identified a major division in scientific opinion that exists on the issues of advocacy and objectivity, highlighting important differences between natural scientists and social scientists. There seem to be three views on these issues which, on reflection, are logically consistent and emerge from the tabular results as well as the specific comments of those interviewed.

One view is that advocacy is acceptable because individual scientists can be objective and because science can be kept separate from policy making. Thus there are no fears that advocacy by individual scientists will contaminate the objectivity on which all scientists depend. A large majority of natural scientists and a significant minority of social scientists interviewed for this study hold this view.[2] Social scientists tend to believe that objectivity is protected more by the scientific process of peer review than by individual integrity.

A second view is predominant among natural scientists who disapprove of advocacy and tend to believe that since it is not possible to separate science and policy making, advocacy will hurt objectivity. Thus they oppose advocacy because they want to retain objectivity, which they see as central to their legitimacy and their mission as scientists.

A third view is most common among social scientists, who begin with suspicions about objectivity and conclude that science cannot be separated from policy making. Thus, for many social scientists, advocacy makes sense because they already see themselves as an important part of the policy process (not separate from it), and believe their task is to retain as much objectivity as they can. They share a less idealistic and more pragmatic approach, which in a way makes them more compatible with the world of the policy maker, and might make them better able to influence policy. In contrast, natural scientists who believe in objectivity are more likely to be upset about not being listened to, or about the failure of scientific knowledge to affect policy.

In sum, the interviews reveal three basic positions on the issues of objectivity, advocacy, and the separation of science and policy that reflect the range of opinions offered throughout the scholarly literature: advocates, separatists, and pragmatists. Advocates believe both that advocacy is acceptable because it is possible to separate science from policy making and that, at least through the scientific process, scientists can remain objective. Separatists believe that advocacy is not acceptable because it is not possible for individual scientists to separate science and policy making and that hence those who advocate lose all semblance of objectivity. Pragmatists believe that advocacy is acceptable because science can never be separated from policy making, so scientists should just do the very best they can to balance objectivity with influence.

More important, the interview results (as defined by the three basic positions delineated above) empirically confirmed that a variation exists across the natural science versus social science disciplines. Natural scientists tend to fall into the category of advocates or separatists and social scientists tend to fall into the category of pragmatists. This finding, that scientific opinion is divided by disciplines, has important implications with respect to the idea of linking science to policy.

First, it suggests that many natural scientists remain a long way from accepting the fact that their research is (or has to be) tainted by the value constraints that characterize the world of policy making. They refuse to compromise the canons of the scientific process and continue to resist entering the policy process in any manner. The upside to this finding (at least for those who believe that objectivity is a worthy ideal) is that a good many natural scientists are fighting to keep their work strictly within the confines of the scientific process. The downside to this finding (at least for those striving to make science more policy-relevant) is that there exists a large number of natural scientists incapable of or unwilling to join science to policy in a meaningful manner.

A second implication of the interview results is that the key to making science more relevant may lie in some type of liaison between natural scientists and social scientists. Social scientists' pragmatic views on objectivity and advocacy align more closely with that of policy makers and allow them to fit more easily into the policy world. Perhaps it is time for those who are interested in fostering better communication between scientists and policy makers to take a harder look at the dialogue occurring between natural scientists and social scientists.

MOVING TOWARD A BETTER DIALOGUE

The Science-Policy Interface

One of the scientists interviewed for this study observed that policy makers are still making decisions without science because study of the science-policy interface is so impoverished. In this regard, he lamented the fact that no one has seriously attempted to define and explain the intricacies of this interface. That may be changing. Recent scholarly work centering on environmental policy making has suggested that a respectful social attitude of scientists and policy makers toward each other in their working relationship may be more important than any differences in orientation that might otherwise divide them (Wilkening 1997, 12). It has also been suggested that the key to improving the linkage of science to policy lies in how scientists connect to the world outside the scientific community (Gregory and Miller 1998, 1).

There is a growing recognition (among scholars) that scientists can no longer work in isolation or just for one side or the other of a policy debate (Schaefer 1998). The connection between scientists and policy makers is no longer viewed as simply a one-to-one relationship between "wise scientists advising independent leaders" (Winstanley et al. 1998, 56). Rather, policy decisions are viewed as products combining public opinion with scientific opinion and reflecting the fact that decision makers are simply representative of the broader public. More and more scientists are being asked to keep their findings and determinations open to examination and challenge. In other words, "[there] should be no domain of science quarantined from public scrutiny. Scientists working in the public sector have a professional and personal responsibility to encourage rigorous self-examination of their own technical judgments in light of their vulnerability to social bias" (Rosenbaum 1998, 137).

At least with respect to environmental issues, there also appears to be much more attention paid to the role that science plays. For instance, in speaking about what makes the environmental policy domain so special, William Leiss stated:

Almost every aspect in this area is presented to politicians and the public in the form of a more or less adequate scientific description of a state of affairs . . . and the adequacy and credibility of that description becomes a key factor—often, *the* key factor—in the policy response. In other words, a great deal of the policy response is a matter of "managing" these scientific descriptions and describing in what way they do (or do not) demand a response that will limit the ability of some social actors to do this or that in a way of creating environmental impacts. (1996, 124)

For the issue of acid rain, Leiss' words ring true. The conflict between scientists and policy makers (as well as among scientists themselves) had more to do with battles over how the science was framed in the policy arena than over the science itself.

The interviews clearly demonstrated that there is a genuine and legitimate fear among natural scientists that the very thing that makes them special and defines their worth in the policy-making process—their commitment to the canons of the scientific method—is being engulfed by a tide of politicization. The core grievance of many of the natural scientists interviewed for this study appears to be that the policy makers do not understand their science and therefore often misuse it, sometimes ignoring science, sometimes twisting it to meet their own values and needs, and sometimes listening but neither understanding nor acting.

This circumstance can be at least partially attributed to the fact that scientists and policy makers come from different institutional environments and have differing sets of values and outlooks, which affect how they view the science and the policy parts of the science-policy linkage. Political culture, societal values, and the governmental institutions and electoral structures within which they operate affect the outlooks of policy makers. Scientists, however, are affected by their own sets of scientific values and norms as well as by university or government institutions and the incentive structures within them. While these worlds overlap, they are largely separate, and this seems to have led to communication problems and the hard feelings between scientists and policy makers in the debate over acid rain.

I would argue that this gap between scientists and policy makers is not going to be closed soon, if ever. Scientists and policy makers do work in separate worlds defined by their own particular logic and understanding. Politics has dominated, and will continue to dominate all aspects of the linkage of science to policy. Once that is understood by all who wish to participate in the policy process, progress can be made toward improving the ways in which science is perceived and used within the policy arena. Furthermore, scientists must understand that simply presenting their scientific findings is not enough to force policy makers to act.

Two instances in the acid rain debate illustrate this point. First, when some of the most well-respected acid rain scientists put together the comprehensive report, *Is There Scientific Consensus on Acid Rain?*, which established (at least in their view) that there was more than enough scientific evidence to begin acid rain controls, the expectation was that policy makers would act. They did not. Second, when scientists were first able to show that there would be economic costs associated with the failure to act, there was the expectation, once again, that policy makers would act. They did not.

In both these instances, scientists failed to account for the complex workings of the environmental policy-making process. Scientists did not take into consideration the fact that policy makers often seek more than just the scientific evidence; they seek some sort of political, social, or economic gain. Scientists also underestimated the importance of a focusing event or a policy entrepreneur or a strong lobbying effort in framing a policy issue. In the end, it was just too easy for policy makers to play scientists against one another, resulting in policy stalemate (or inaction).

As it turns out, William Leiss was right. The key to making good environmental policy may well rest with the clarity with which scientists are able to frame their scientific findings and scientists would do well to pay more attention to that aspect of the science-policy linkage.

The Natural-Social Science Interface

One thing that was made very clear by the interview responses is that natural scientists prize their commitment to objectivity as something that cannot be compromised. Thus the question becomes, how can scientists retain their ties to the scientific ideal of objectivity and, at the same time, participate in framing their scientific findings in a way that makes them more accessible to the policy world? The answer, I believe, must come from within the scientific community itself.

In fact, the key may lie not in the dialogue between scientists and policy makers, but in the dialogue between natural scientists and social scientists. Why is the interaction between these two disciplines within the scientific community so important to the environmental policy-making process? One reason is that natural scientists continue to be very reluctant to enter the policy-making process. For natural scientists, there exist strong ties to the tenets of the scientific process that run counter to any type of policy advocacy. Yet, natural scientists also appear very frustrated because the good science does not seem to be getting into the policy debate. Natural scientists find themselves in a quandary. If they advocate for specific policy outcomes, they risk losing their highly valued credibility within the scientific community. If they do not advocate, they become policy-irrelevant.

Social scientists could help alleviate this particular dilemma. They could play a mediating role, helping policy makers understand the intricacies of the scientific process and helping natural scientists to clarify their own personal biases. Social scientists could also contribute by providing better explanations (hopefully, leading to a better understanding) of such important concepts as environment, health, clean air, cost, truth, uncertainty, and so on. Simply put, social scientists have special expertise in framing issues. That is exactly where their training lies. They study the policy process, understand the ways it operates, and are in an ideal position to frame environmental science in a way that would make it more accessible to those—including many policy makers— who do not have a clear grasp of the way science works. If social scientists were to be used as conduits between natural scientists and policy makers, it is possible that the science could move forward with more clarity and natural scientists could preserve their relative independence and objectivity from further erosion.

Certainly, the tensions between natural scientists and social scientists are well documented. Bridging the gap between these two separate disciplines in the scientific community may be just as difficult as bridging the gap between scientists and policy makers. However, there is room for optimism because there is a growing recognition among natural scientists that they must do a better job of incorporating aspects of the social sciences into their work. Eville Gorham summarized this view.

It seems to me as a scientist that the overriding problem we face lies in the contrast between the relative simplicity of the physical sciences and the extreme complexity of the social sciences. . . . Advances in the enormously complex social sciences that undergrid economics, politics, law and management have necessarily come much more slowly than advances in technology, and so have been largely—though not entirely—unsuccessful in devising policies and procedures to arrest and ameliorate the ever-increasing ecological degradation caused by technological change. (1997, 30–31)

Along these lines, there is now a recurring call for closer collaboration between natural scientists and social scientists, the goal being social scientists' full acceptance as partners in the process of focusing science on social problems (Gregory and Miller 1998, 248–50; Pielke 1997, 262; Sclove 1998, B4). The findings of this study support that view.

The interviews illustrated the scientific community's frustration as well as its hope for bringing natural scientists and policy makers closer together. The frustration lies in the fact that most natural scientists perceive that the results of their scientific studies are not getting through to policy makers in a way that effectively defines the science as it applies to environmental policy formation. Furthermore, there is a tendency, at times, to blame policy makers alone for this adverse situation. The hope lies in the fact that there appear to be more and more natural scientists looking within their own ranks for answers for these perceived problems. Many of the natural scientists interviewed put the blame squarely on scientists themselves for not personally taking the time or making the effort to put their scientific findings in a context more assessable and understandable to the nonscientific world, meaning policy makers and the public at large.

The major stumbling block to making this connection to the policy world rests with natural scientists' strong belief that they can remain both objective in their work and separate from the politics that dominate the policy process. Many natural scientists continue to believe that they can be both scientists and citizen activists at the same time. The truth is, natural scientists stand alone in this conviction. Neither social scientists nor policy makers accept this view. The continued use of science to support ideological bents (on all sides of an issue) and the growing tendency to shop for scientists that support specific policy positions testify to the fact that natural scientists must rethink how they fit into the policy process. Natural scientists must come to the full realization that there needs to be a middle ground between the advocacy and the separatist positions. As the acid rain debate clearly demonstrated, both of these positions have serious drawbacks in terms of linking science to policy. If a scientist becomes just another party to the cause, he or she risks losing credibility within both the scientific community and the policy arena. If a scientist remains aloof from the policy world, he or she risks becoming irrelevant to the policy process.

Ultimately, all scientists must realize that their divisions of opinion on objectivity, advocacy, and the separation of science from policy hurt the credibility of all scientists as they enter the realm of policy making. Policy makers can play on the divisions among scientists to discredit views with which they do not agree, and to shop for scientific knowledge that supports their political bent. Coming to some type of consensus on the acceptable boundaries of advocacy and the true nature of objectivity would allow the scientists themselves to communicate better with policy makers. This would give both scientists and policy makers a better sense of when and how to use scientific knowledge in the policy process, or—in short—how to best make the science to policy linkage.

Finally, to achieve this consensus, scientists should initiate a dialog between the natural and social science disciplines. Scientists need to educate each other so that they can present a united front to policy makers on the issue of when scientists and scientific information is objective and when it is not. This would allow bad science to be easily identified by all participants in the policy process, and it would strengthen the legitimacy of scientific knowledge that is used in forming policy. These recommendations are made with the knowledge that such a dialog already exits in many places, but with hope that more attention will be given to these disciplinary divisions.

SOME CONCLUDING THOUGHTS

In the final analysis, scientists can take much of the credit for keeping the acid rain issue alive and for ensuring that acid rain remained an enduring policy issue on the United States governmental agenda. However, scientists must also take stock of the cost. Crossing the boundary that separates scientists from the policy world was relatively easy to do for those scientists who chose to do so. Furthermore, the story of acid rain (as depicted by this work) suggests that scientists who became policy advocates did have an immediate and lasting impact on the acid rain debate. But because so many scientists did choose to advocate, there now appears to be a genuine question about whether these scientists are now recognized (or welcome) within the scientific community as a whole. As Dorothy Nelkin observed: "[T]he willingness of scientists to lend their expertise to various factions in widely publicized disputes has undermined assumptions about the objectivity of science, and these are precisely the assumptions that have given scientists their power as the neutral arbiters of truth" (1995, 453).

Nelkin's words were written as part of an analysis attempting to explain the increasing use of science as a forum to contest deeply held values in American society and not as an indictment of the science of acid rain. But her words readily apply to the part that scientists played in the acid rain debate. And, unfortunately for some scientists, the lasting impact of their participation in the acid rain debate may not be the critical role they played in bringing about a reduction in acid rain pollutants. Rather, these scientists may be best remembered for forsaking the tenets of good science that serve as both the foundation and the moral compass of the scientific process.

Having said all that, it is important to remember that the concerns about acid rain, the environment, and the workings of the science-policy nexus are not going away any time soon. First of all, acid rain continues to be viewed as a serious and important problem by many within the scientific communities of the United States and Canada. Acid rain has recently been linked to several other environmental stresses in North America. Scientists have been reporting that acid rain is intimately connected to such environmental concerns as climate warming, the increasing exposure to ultraviolet radiation, and to the depletion of stratospheric ozone (Gorham 1996, 109; Schindler et al. 1996, 705–7; Winstanley et al. 1998, 54; Yan et al. 1996, 141–43). Some scientists are also now arguing that the 1990 Clean Air Act Amendments have proven inadequate to protect our surface waters and forest soils against further anthropogenic acidification (Likens, Driscoll, and Buso 1996, 247).

Second, the problems encountered in the acid rain debate are being played out all over again in the policy debate over climate change. Carefully read two recent exerpts from publications about climate change:

• Atmospheric scientists are traditionally so cautious in their statements, it is the extreme arguments of hired-gun skeptics which appear more authoritative in a public arena. This is particularly true in the United States, where heated debate is often the preferred medium of discussion. (Dunn 1998, 35)

• The inability of scientists to offer [a] consensus produced a public-relations fiasco for the American Geophysical Union. . . . In a statement released at a packed news conference, the organization tried to clarify to the public the position of its members on climate change and rising levels of greenhouse gases. But the convoluted wording of its statements . . . only led to more confusion among reporters about how scientists really view climate change. (McDonald 1999, A18)

To be sure, establishing the line between science and policy (if such a line exists) is wrought with complexity, because policy making involves making value judgments. While some contend that value judgments belong only in the realm of politics, others maintain that this is simply an impossibility—that value judgments pervade all levels of decision making, including those of scientists. Because the perception exists that political values permeate all scientific endeavors, it has been difficult for scientists to persuade both policy makers and the public at large that their findings provide an accurate description of environmental conditions. This has been especially true of the policy debate over acid rain.

In fact, the story of how acid rain legislation came about in the United States serves as an excellent illustration of how the debate over the credibility of science (and scientists) can permeate (and sometimes overwhelm) the actual policy debate over environmental issues. The scientists and policy makers involved in today's environmental policy debates would do well to reflect on ways to learn from the experiences of the past, because the importance of the science-policy linkage to environmental policy making is sure to continue well into the 21st century. Scientists, especially, must continue to strive to find ways that they—as a whole—can identify the extent of scientific consensus that exists on an issue at a given time and communicate that consensus to policy makers in a way that makes sense to the policy world but still remains true to the tenets of the scientific process.

NOTES

1. Along these lines, John Carroll argued that "[w]idespread atmospheric acid pollution must increasingly be viewed as a threat to national sovereignty and, indeed, to the very notion of the nation-state in its fundamental role of protecting the citizenry within its own border[s]" (1990, 2).

2. Table 5.2 shows that the majority of natural scientists think that science can be separate from policy making, while the majority of social scientists disagree. Table 6.2 shows that the majority of natural scientists think that scientists can be objective, while social scientists are much more skeptical, with only a slim majority believing objectivity is possible (including those who think that it is possible within the scientific process).

Bibliography

Ackerman, Bruce, and William Hassler. 1981. *Clean Coal/Dirty Air*. New Haven: Yale University Press.

Alm, Leslie R. 1988–89. "Scientists, Researchers, and Acid Rain." *Journal of Environmental Systems* 18:265–77.

_____. 1990. "The United States–Canadian Acid Rain Debate: The Science-Politics Linkage." *American Review of Canadian Studies* 20:59–79.

_____. 1990. "Across Borders: International Influences on Domestic Agenda Building." *Journal of Borderlands Studies* 5:265–77.

_____. 1993. "The Long Road Toward Influence: Canada as an American Interest Group." *Journal of Borderlands Studies* 8:13–32.

_____. 1994. "Acid Rain and the Key Factors of Issue Maintenance." *The Environmental Professional* 16:254–61.

_____. 1994–95. "Policy Elite Perceptions: Canada, the United States and Acid Rain." *Journal of Environmental Systems* 23:97–108.

_____. 1997. "Scientists and the Acid Rain Policy in Canada and the United States." *Science, Technology, & Human Values* 22:349–68.

Alm, Leslie R., and Charles Davis. 1993. "Agenda Setting and Acid Precipitation in the United States." *Environmental Management* 17:807–16.

Ashford, Nicholas A. 1995. "Re: Disclosure of Interest: A Time for Clarity." *American Journal of Industrial Medicine* 28:611–12.

Barton, Richard. 1990. *Ties That Bind in Canadian/American Relations: Politics of News Discourse*. Hillsdale, New Jersey: Lawrence Erlbaum Associates.

Baumgartner, Frank, and Bryan Jones. 1993. *Agenda and Instability in American Politics*. Chicago: The University of Chicago Press.

Beardsley, Erik. 1987. "Director of Acid Rain Report Quits Under Scientists' Fire." *Fort Collins (Colorado) Collegian*, October 1, p. 7.

Begley, Sharon, and Mary Hager. 1986. "Acid Rain's 'Fingerprints.'" *Newsweek*, August 11.

Bimber, Bruce. 1996. *The Politics of Expertise in Congress: The Rise and Fall of the Office of Technology Assessment.* Albany: State University of New York Press.

Bocking, Stephen. 1997. *Ecologists and Environmental Politics: A History of Contemporary Ecology.* New Haven: Yale University Press.

Brown, George E., Jr. 1997. "Environmental Science Under Siege in the U.S. Congress." *Environment* 39:13–31.

Brown, Susan. 1981. "International–United States Air Pollution Control and the Acid Rain Phenomenon." *Natural Resources Journal* 21:631–45.

Bryner, Gary. 1995. *Blue Skies, Green Politics: The Clean Air Act of 1990 and Its Implementation.* Washington, D.C.: CQ Press.

Caldwell, Lynton K. 1985. "Binational Responsibilities for a Shared Environment." In *Canada and the United States: Enduring Friendship, Persistent Stress,* eds. Charles F. Doran and John H. Sigler. Englewood Cliffs, New Jersey: Prentice Hall.

Canada. House of Commons. Committee on Fisheries and Forestry, Subcommittee on Acid Rain. 1981. *Still Waters.* 32nd Parliament, 1st sess.

Carroll, John. 1982. *Acid Rain: An Issue in Canadian-American Relations.* Washington, D.C.: National Planning Association.

————. 1986. *Environmental Diplomacy: An Examination and a Prospective of Canadian–U.S. Transboundary Environmental Relations.* Ann Arbor: The University of Michigan Press.

————. 1990. *Transboundary Air Quality Relations.* Canadian-American Public Policy, no. 2. Orono, Maine: The Canadian-American Center.

————. 1991. "Environmental Issues and Future Canadian Policy." In *Canada and the United States in the 1990s: An Emerging Partnership,* ed. William Winegard. Washington, D.C.: Brassey's.

Cataldo, Everett. 1992. "Acid Rain Policy in the United States: An Exploration of Canadian Influence." *The Social Science Journal* 29:395–409.

Chamberlin, Alice, and Leonard Legault. 1997. "International Joint Commission Looks to the 21st Century." *Focus* 22:3–5.

Chapin, Paul. 1988. "State of Canada/U.S. Relations." Presented at Seminar on United States–Canadian Relations, United States Air Force Academy, Colorado Springs, Colorado.

Clarkson, Stephen. 1983. "Congress and the Foreign Lobbies." Presented at the School of Advanced International Studies, Johns Hopkins University, Baltimore, Maryland.

Cohen, Michael, James March, and Johan Olsen. 1972. "A Garbage Can Model of Organizational Choice." *Administrative Science Quarterly* 17:1–25.

Cohen, Richard E. 1995. *Washington at Work: Back Rooms and Clean Air.* Boston: Allyn and Bacon.

Cole, K.C., and Robert Hotz. 1999. "Rapid Spread of Information Distorts Scientific Discoveries." *Idaho Statesman,* January 24, p. 4A.

Cole, Leonard A. 1993. *Element of Risk: The Politics of Radon.* New York: Oxford University Press.

Collingridge, David, and Colin Reeve. 1986. *Science Speaks to Power: The Role of Experts in Policy Making.* New York: St. Martin's Press.

Cook, Mary Etta, and Roger Davidson. 1985. "Deferral Politics: Congressional Decision Making on Environmental Issues in the 1980s." In *Public Policy and the Natural Environment,* eds. Helen Ingram and R. Kenneth Godwin. Greenwich, Connecticut: JAI Press Inc.

Cowling, Ellis B. 1982. "Acid Precipitation in Historical Perspective." *Environmental Science and Technology* 16:110–23A.

_____. 1988. "Role of Scientists and Other Scholars in Public Decision Making." Presented at a Seminar on Ethics in Graduate Education sponsored by the Graduate School at North Carolina State University.

_____. 1992. "The Performance and Legacy of NAPAP." *Ecological Applications* 2:111–16.

Cozzens Susan E., and Edward J. Woodhouse. 1995. "Science, Government and the Politics of Knowledge." In *Handbook of Science and Technology Studies*, eds. Sheila Jasanoff, Gerald E. Markle, James C. Peterson, and Trevor Pinch. Thousand Oaks, California: Sage Publications.

CQ Almanac. 1979. "Energy/Environment." 35:603.

Crandall, Robert. 1984. "An Acid Test for Congress." *Regulation* 8:21–28.

Curtis, Kenneth M., and John E. Carroll. 1983. *Canadian-American Relations: The Promise and the Challenge.* Lexington, Massachusetts: D.C. Heath and Company.

Daily, Gretchen. 1997. *Nature's Services: Societal Dependence on Natural Ecosystems.* Washington, D.C.: Island Press.

Davis, David. 1982. *Energy Politics.* 3rd Edition. New York: St. Martin's Press.

Davis, Joseph. 1982a. "Talks Seek End to Impasse Over Clean Air Act Rewrite." *Congressional Quarterly Weekly Report* 40:1347.

_____. 1982b. "EPA and Congress at Odds Over Budget, Policy Issues." *Congressional Quarterly Weekly Report* 40:1827–30.

_____. 1983a. "Acid Rain Still a Sore Point for United States, Canada: But Both Sides Are Optimistic." *Congressional Quarterly Weekly Report* 41:1063–65.

_____. 1983b. "No Reagan Acid Rain Legislation in Sight." *Congressional Quarterly Weekly Report* 41:2186–87.

_____. 1984. "Clean Air Reauthorization With New Acid Rain Controls Approved by Senate Panel." *Congressional Quarterly Weekly Report* 42:621–22.

_____. 1985. "Reagan Gave OMB a Regulatory Veto, But Decision is Being Tested in Court." *Congressional Quarterly Weekly Report* 43:1816–17.

_____. 1986. "Acid Rain to Get Attention as Reagan Changes Course." *Congressional Quarterly Weekly Report* 44:675–76.

_____. 1988. "All Sides Blamed for Death of Clean-Air Bill." *Congressional Quarterly Weekly Report* 46:2812.

Denver Post. 1987. "Reagan Acid Rain Report Fails Litmus Test." September 27, pp. F1–F3.

Diemer, Tom. 1989. "Cloud Over Acid Rain May Be Shifting." *Cleveland Plain Dealer*, February 12, p. A1.

Doran, Charles. 1997. "Style as a Substitute for Issue Articulation in Canada–U.S. Relations." *The American Review of Canadian Studies* 27:167–78.

Dowd, Maureen. 1989. "Bush in Ottawa, Now Vows to Pursue Acid Rain Pact." *New York Times*, February 11, p. A3.

Driscoll, Charles, Gene Likens, Lars Hedin, John Eaton, and F. Herbert Bormann. 1989. "Changes in the Chemistry of Surface Waters." *Environment, Science, and Technology* 23:137–43.

Driscoll, Charles, James Galloway, James Hornig, Gene Likens, Michael Oppenheimer, Kenneth Rahn, and David Schindler. 1985. *Is There Scientific Consensus on Acid Rain?* Millbrook, New York: Institute of Ecosystem Studies.

Dunn, Seth. 1998. "Clearing the Haze." *World Watch* 11:35–6.

Enman, Charles. 1997. "When Science, Politics Collide." *The Ottawa (Ontario) Citizen*, July 12, p. B1.

The Environmental Professional. 1994. "Linkages are Weak Between Science and Environmental Decisionmaking." 16:111–21.

EPA Journal. 1991. "Preface." 17(1): 1.

Finkel, Adam M., and Dominic Golding. 1994. *Worst Things First? The Debate Over Risk-Based National Environmental Priorities*. Washington, D.C.: Resources for the Future.

Forster, Bruce. 1993. *The Acid Rain Debate: Scientists and Special Interests in Policy Formation*. Ames: Iowa State University Press.

Franklin, Claire, Richard Burnett, Richard Paolini, and Mark Raizenne. 1985. "Health Risks From Acid Rain: A Canadian Perspective." *Environmental Health Perspectives* 63:155–68.

Freeman, George, Jr. 1985. "The U.S. Politics of Acid Rain." In *The Acid Rain Debate: Scientific, Economic, and Political Dimensions*, eds. Ernest J. Yanarella and Randal H. Ihara. Boulder: Westview Press.

Fry, Earl. 1988. "State of Canada/U.S. Relations." Seminar on United States–Canadian Relations at the United States Air Force Academy, Colorado Springs, Colorado.

Gerdel, Thomas. 1989. "Cloud Over Coal Country." *Cleveland Plain Dealer*, June 25, p. C1.

Gibian, Glenn. 1985. "Predicting Deposition Reductions Using Long-Range Transport Models: Some Policy Implications." In *The Acid Rain Debate: Scientific, Economic, and Political Dimensions*, eds. Ernest J. Yanarella and Randal H. Ihara. Boulder: Westview Press.

Glode, Mark, and Beverly Nelson Glode. 1993. "Transboundary Pollution: Acid Rain and United States–Canadian Relations." *Boston College Environmental Affairs Law Review* 20:1–35.

Gorham, Eville. 1996. "Lakes Under a Three-pronged Attack." *Nature* 381:109–10.

_____. 1997. "Human Impacts on Ecosystems and Landscapes." In *Placing Nature: Culture and Landscape Ecology*, ed. J. I. Nassauer. Washington, D.C.: Island Press.

Gorrie, Peter. 1990. "How the Acid-Rain Battle Was Begun." *Toronto Star*, November 18, p. C1.

Gould, Roy. 1985. *Going Sour: Science and Politics of Acid Rain*. Boston: Birkhauser.

Graham, John D., Laura C. Green, and Marc J. Roberts. 1988. *In Search of Safety: Chemicals and Cancer Risk*. Cambridge: Harvard University Press.

Gregory, Jane, and Steve Miller. 1998. *Science in Public: Communication, Culture, and Credibility*. New York: Plenum Press.

Hagan, William, Jr. 1994. "Culture Wars." *Science* 265:853–54.

Hager, George. 1989a. "Acid-Rain Controls Advance on Both Sides of Aisle." *Congressional Quarterly Weekly Report* 47:688–91.

_____. 1989b. "Energy Panel Seals Pact on Vehicle Pollution." *Congressional Quarterly Weekly Report* 47:2621–24.

_____. 1990. "The 'White House Effect' Opens a Long-Locked Political Door." *Congressional Quarterly Weekly Report* 48:139–44.

Hamlett, Patrick W. 1992. *Understanding Technological Politics: A Decision-Making Approach*. Englewood Cliffs, New Jersey: Prentice Hall.

Harrison, Kathryn, and George Hoberg. 1994. *Risk, Science, and Politics: Regulating Toxic Substances in Canada and the United States*. Montreal: McGill-Queen's University Press.

Harsha, Barbara. 1983. "Controlling Acid Rain: Pro and Con." A Policy Working Paper for the National League of Cities. Washington, D.C.

Holsti, K. J. 1971. "Canada and the United States." In *Conflict in World Politics*, eds. Steven Spiegel and Kenneth Waltz. Cambridge: Winthrop Publishers, Inc.

Ihara, Randal. 1985. "An Overview of the Acid Rain Debate: Politics, Science, and the Search for Consensus." In *The Acid Rain Debate: Scientific, Economic, and Political Dimensions*, eds. Ernest J. Yanarella and Randall H. Ihara. Boulder: Westview Press.

Ingram, Helen, H. Brinton Milward, and Wendy Laird. 1990. "Scientists and Agenda Setting: Advocacy and Global Warming." Presented at the annual meeting of the Western Political Science Association, Newport Beach, California.

Israelson, David. 1990. *Silent Earth: The Politics of Our Survival*. Toronto: Penguin Books.

Jasanoff, Sheila. 1990. *The Fifth Branch: Science Advisors as Policymakers*. Cambridge: Harvard University Press.

Jockel, Joseph. 1990. *Canadian-American Policy: Canada–U.S. Relations in the Bush Era*. Canadian-American Public Policy, no. 1. Orono, Maine: The Canadian-American Center.

Johnson, Janet. 1985. "The Dynamics of Acid Rain Policy in the United States." In *Public Policy and the Natural Environment*, eds. Helen Ingram and R. Kenneth Godwin. Greenwich, Connecticut: JAI Press Inc.

Jones, Lilias, Pamela Duncan, and Stephen Mumme. 1997. "Assessing Transboundary Environmental Impacts on the U.S.–Mexican and U.S.–Canadian Borders." *Journal of Borderlands Studies* 12:73–96.

Jones, Megan, David H. Guston, and Lewis M. Branscomb. 1996. *Informed Legislatures: Coping With Science in a Democracy*. Cambridge: Harvard University Press.

Kahan, Archie. 1986. *Acid Rain: Reign of Controversy*. Golden, Colorado: Fulcrum, Inc.

Kenski, Henry, and Margaret Kenski. 1984. "Congress Against the President: The Struggle Over the Environment." In *Environmental Policy in the 1980s: Reagan's New Agenda*, eds. Norman Vig and Michael Kraft. Washington, D.C.: Congressional Quarterly Inc.

Kerr, Richard. 1982. "Tracing Sources of Acid Rain Causes Big Stir." *Science* 215: 881.

Kingdon, John W. 1995. *Agendas, Alternatives, and Public Policies*. 2nd edition. New York: Harper Collins College Publishers.

Kirton, John. 1993. "A Global Partnership: The Canada–United States Political Relationship in the 1990s." In *Handbooks to the Modern World: Canada*, ed. Mel Watkins. New York: Facts on File.

Koch, Kathy. 1980a. "Conversion Seen Adding Little to Pollution." *Congressional Quarterly Weekly Report* 38:1486–87.

_____. 1980b. "Dealing With Environmental Health Effects of Coal Use." *Congressional Quarterly Weekly Report* 38:1488–89.

_____. 1980c. "Pollutants From Coal Burning Plants and the Spread of Acid Rainfall." *Congressional Quarterly Weekly Report* 38:1490–91.

Kriz, Margaret. 1990. "Dunning the Midwest." *National Journal* 22:893–7.

Kurtz, Howard. 1991. "Is Acid Rain a Tempest in News Media Teapot?" *Washington Post*, January 14, 1991, p. A3.

LaBastille, Anne. 1979. "The Killing Rains." *Garden* 3:9–13.

_____. 1981. "Acid Rain: How Great a Menace?" *National Geographic* 160:652–81.

Lackey, Robert T., and Roger L. Blair. 1997. "Science, Policy, and Acid Rain." *Renewable Resources Journal* 13:9–13.

LaFranchi, Howard. 1987. "Acid Rain, Associated With the Northeast, Crops Up in Texas." *Christian Science Monitor*, September 16, p. 6.

Lee, Kai N. 1993. *Compass and Gyroscope: Integrating Science and Politics for the Environment.* Washington, D.C.: Island Press.

Leiss, William. 1996. "Governance and the Environment." In *Policy Frameworks for a Knowledge Economy*, ed. T. Courchene. Kingston, Ontario: John Deutsch Institute for the Study of Economic Policy.

Lewis, Drew, and William Davis. 1986. *Joint Report of the Special Envoys.* Washington, D.C.: U.S. Government Printing Office.

Leyton-Brown, David, and Christopher Sands. 1997. "Introduction." *The American Review of Canadian Studies* 27:163–66.

Lichtinger, Victor. 1997. "Foreword." *Continental Pollutant Pathways.* Montreal: Commission for Environmental Cooperation.

Likens, Gene. 1976. "Acid Precipitation." *Chemical and Engineering News* 54:29–44.

_____. 1989. "Some Aspects of Air Pollutant Effects on Terrestrial Ecosystems and Prospects for the Future." *Ambrio* 18:172–78.

Likens, Gene, C.T. Driscoll, and D.C. Buso. 1996. "Long-Term Effects of Acid Rain: Response and Recovery of a Forest Ecosystem." *Science* 272:244–47.

Likens, Gene, F. Herbert Bormann, and Noye Johnson. 1972. "Acid Rain." *Environment* 14:33–40.

Likens, Gene, Richard Wright, James Galloway, and Thomas Butler. 1979. "Acid Rain." *Scientific American* 241:43–51.

Litfin, Karen T. 1994. *Ozone Discourses: Science and Politics in Global Environmental Cooperation.* New York: Columbia University Press.

Loucks, Orie L. 1993. "Science or Politics? NAPAP and Reagan." *Forum for Applied Research and Public Policy* 8:66–72.

Lubchenco, Jane. 1998. "Entering the Century of the Environment: A New Social Contract for Science." *Science* 279:491–97.

Lynn, Frances M. 1986. "The Interplay of Science and Values in Assessing and Regulating Environmental Risks." *Science, Technology, & Human Values* 11:40–50.

Macdonald, Doug. 1997. "Two-Level Games and the Federated State: Federal-Provincial Negotiation of the Canadian Cost of Acid Rain Controls." Presented at the annual meeting of the International Studies Association, Toronto, Canada.

Mangun, William. 1995. "Why Acid Rain Bills Did Not Become Law: The Role of Scientists, Lobbyists, and the Courts." *Research in Public Policy Analysis and Management* 6:25–48.

Marshall, Eliot. 1982 "Air Pollution Clouds U.S.–Canadian Relations." *Science* 217:1118–19.

McDonald, Kim. 1999. "Scientists Falter in Bid to Explain Stance on Climate Change." *Chronicle of Higher Education* XLI(22): A18.

McKinsey, Lauren, and Victor Konrad. 1989. *Borderlands Reflections: The United States and Canada.* Orono, Maine: The Canadian-American Center.

Meyer, Richard, and Bruce Yandle. 1987. "The Political Economy of Acid Rain." *Cato Journal* 7:527–45.

Meyer, Stephen. 1995. "The Role of Scientists in the 'New Politics.'" *Chronicle of Higher Education* XLI(37): B1–B2.

Mitchell, Robert. 1984. "Public Opinion and Environmental Politics in the 1970s and 1980s." In *Environmental Policy in the 1980s: Reagan's New Agenda,* eds. Norman Vig and Michael Kraft. Washington, D.C.: Congressional Quarterly Inc.

Mohnen, Volker. 1988. "The Challenge of Acid Rain." *Scientific American* 259:30–38.

Mosher, Lawrence. 1981a. "Acid Drizzle." *National Journal* 13:1301.

_____. 1981b. "Courting Trouble." *National Journal* 13:1996.

_____. 1982. "Clean Air Supporters Are Outflanked by Sponsors of a 'Bipartisan Bill.'" *National Journal* 14:237–40.

_____. 1983a. "Acid Rain Debate May Play a Role in the 1984 Presidential Sweepstakes." *National Journal* 15:998–99.

_____. 1983b. "Administration Loses Its Umbrella Against Steadfast Acid Rain Policy." *National Journal* 15:1590–91.

Munton, Don. 1980–81. "Dependence and Interdependence in Trans-boundary Environmental Relations." *International Journal* 36:139–84.

_____. 1981. "Acid Rain and Basic Politics." *Alternatives* 10:21–28.

_____. 1983. "Diplomacy Under Constraint: Life, Liberty and the American Pursuit of Acid Rain." *Alternatives* 11:13–20.

_____. 1997a. "Acid Rain and Transboundary Air Quality in Canadian-American Relations." *The American Review of Canadian Studies* 27:327–58.

_____. 1997b. "The Ideas of Regimes: Changing Environmental and Political Thinking on Acid Rain Controls." Presented at the annual meeting of the International Studies Association, Toronto, Canada.

Munton, Don, and Geoffrey Castle. 1992. "Air, Water, and Political Fire: Building a North American Environmental Regime." In *Canadian Foreign Policy and International Economic Regimes,* eds. A. Claire Cutler and Mark Zacher. Vancouver: University of British Columbia Press.

Myers, John Peterson, and Joshua S. Reichert. 1997. "Perspectives on Nature's Services." In *Nature's Services: Societal Dependence on Natural Ecosystems,* ed. Gretchen C. Daily. Washington, D.C.: Island Press.

Navarro, Peter. 1981. "The 1977 Clean Air Act Amendments: Energy, Environmental, Economic, and Distributional Impacts." *Public Policy* 29:121–46.

Nelkin, Dorothy. 1995. "Science Controversies: The Dynamics of Public Disputes in the United States." In *Handbook of Science and Technology Studies,* eds. Sheila Jasanoff, Gerald E. Markle, James C. Peterson, and Trevor Pinch. Thousand Oaks, California: Sage Publications.

New, W.H. 1998. *Borderlands.* Vancouver: University of British Columbia Press.

New York Times. 1989. "Transcript of President's Address to a Joint Session of the House and Senate." February 10, p. A17.

New York Times. 1990. "Acid Rain: Plenty Bad Enough." January 29, p. A22.

Nossal, Kim Richard. 1997. "'Without Regard to the Interests of Others': Canada and American Unilateralism in the Post-Cold War Era." *The American Review of Canadian Studies* 27:179–97.

Parker, Larry, and John Blodgett. 1985. "Acid Rain Legislation and the Clean Air Act: Time to Raise the Bridge or Lower the River?" In *The Acid Rain Debate: Scientific, Economic, and Political Dimensions*, eds. Ernest J. Yanarella and Randal H. Ihara. Boulder: Westview Press.

Perhac, Ralph M. 1991a. "Making Credible Science Usable: Lessons From CAA, NAPAP." *Power Engineering* 94:38–40.

———. 1991b. "Usable Science: Lessons From Acid Rain Legislation, NAPAP. *Power Engineering* 94:26–29.

Pielke, Roger, Jr. 1997. "Asking the Right Questions: Atmospheric Sciences Research and Social Needs." *Bulletin of the American Meteorological Society* 78:255–64.

Pierce, John C., Mary Ann Steger, Nicholas Lovrich, and Brent Steel. 1989. "In Bed With the Elephant: Canadian and American Public and Activists' Perceptions of Responsibility for Acid Rain." Presented at the biennial meeting of the Association for Canadian Studies in the United States, San Francisco.

Pierson, William, and T. Y. Chang. 1986. "Acid Rain in Western Europe and the Northeastern United States—A Technical Appraisal." *CRC Critical Reviews in Environmental Control* 16:167–92.

Plutzer, Eric, Ardith Maney, and Robert O'Connor. 1998. "Ideology and Elites' Perceptions of the Safety of New Technologies." *American Journal of Political Science* 42:190–209.

Postel, Sandra. 1985. "Protecting Forests From Air Pollution and Acid Rain." In *State of the World, 1985*, ed. Lester R. Brown. New York: W.W. Norton and Company.

Proctor, Robert N. 1991. *Value-Free Science? Purity and Power in Modern Knowledge*. Cambridge: Harvard University Press.

Pytte, Alyson. 1990. "A Decade's Acrimony Lifted in the Glow of Clean Air." *Congressional Quarterly Weekly Report* 48:3587–92.

Regens, James. 1984. "Acid Rain and Public Policy." *Chemtech* 14:310–16.

———. 1985. "The Political Economy of Acid Rain." *Publius: The Journal of Federalism* 15:53–66.

Regens, James, and Robert Rycroft. 1988. *The Acid Rain Controversy*. Pittsburgh: University of Pittsburgh Press.

Reilly, William. 1991. "The New Clean Air Act: An Environmental Milestone." *EPA Journal* 17:2–4.

Rhodes, Steven, and Paulette Middleton. 1983a. "Acid Rain's Gang of Four: More Than One Impact." *The Environmental Forum* 2:32–35.

———. 1983b. "Canada, the U.S., and Acid Rain." *Environment* 25:34–35.

Ringquist, Evan J. 1993. *Environmental Protection at the State Level: Politics and Progress in Controlling Pollution*. Armonk, NY: M.E. Sharp.

———. 1998. "Efficiency vs. Equity in Environmental Protection: Trading SO_2 Emissions Under the 1990 CAA." Presented at the annual meeting of the American Political Science Association, Boston.

Roberts, Leslie. 1987. "Federal Report on Acid Rain Draws Criticism." *Science* 237:1404–6.

———. 1991. "Learning From an Acid Rain Program." *Science* 251:1302–5.

Roeder, Phillip, and Timothy Johnson. 1985. "Public Opinion and the Environment: The Problem of Acid Rain." In *The Acid Rain Debate: Scientific, Economic, and Political Dimensions*, eds. Ernest J. Yanarella and Randal H. Ihara. Boulder: Westview Press.

Rosenbaum, Walter A. 1998. *Environmental Politics and Policy.* 4th Edition. Washington, D.C.: CQ Press.

Rosenberg, William. 1991. "Questions and Answers." *EPA Journal* 17:5–10.

Roth, Philip, Charles Blanchard, John Harte, Harvey Michaels, and Mohamed T. El-Ashry. 1985. *The American West's Acid Rain Test.* Washington, D.C.: World Resources Institute.

Rubin, Edward, Lester Lave, and M. Granger Morgan. 1991–1992. "Keeping Climate Research Relevant." *Issues in Science and Technology* 7:47–55.

Rushefsky, Mark. 1995. "Elites and Environmental Policy." In *Environmental Politics and Policy,* ed. James P. Lester. Durham: Duke University Press.

Russell, Milton. 1992. "Lessons from NAPAP." *Ecological Applications* 2:107–10.

Safina, Carl. 1998. "To Save the Earth, Scientists Should Join Policy Debates." *Chronicle of Higher Education* XLV(2): A80.

Sarewitz, Daniel. 1996. *Frontiers of Illusion: Science, Technology, and the Politics of Progress.* Philadelphia: Temple University Press.

Schaefer, Mark. 1998. "Environmental Conflict Resolution and Negotiation Beyond 'Crisis Diplomacy.'" Presented at the Shared Waters/Shared Stewardship Conference, Western Washington University, Bellingham, Washington.

Schindler, David W. 1992. "A View of NAPAP From North of the Border." *Ecological Applications* 2:124–30.

Schindler, David, P. Jefferson Curtis, Brian Parker, and Michael Stainton. 1996. "Consequences of Climate Warming and Lake Acidification for UV-B Penetration in North American Boreal Lakes." *Nature* 379:705–8.

Schmandt, Jurgen, Judith Clarkson, and Hilliard Roderick. 1988. *Acid Rain and Friendly Neighbors: The Policy Dispute Between Canada and the United States.* 2nd Edition. Durham: Duke University Press.

Schwartz, Alan. 1994. "Canada–U.S. Environmental Relations: A Look at the 1990s." *The American Review of Canadian Studies* 24:489–508.

Sclove, Richard. 1998. "For U.S. Science Policy, It's Time for a Reality Check." *Chronicle of Higher Education* XLV(9): B4.

Shabecoff, Philip. 1988. "Acid Rain Called Peril to Sea Life on Atlantic Coast." *New York Times,* April 25, p. A1.

––––––. 1989. "Clean Air Backers Like Way Wind Is Blowing." *New York Times,* March 7, 1989, p. B6.

Simon, Marc V., and Leslie R. Alm. 1995. "Policy Windows and Two-Level Games: Explaining the Passage of Acid Rain Legislation in the Clean Air Act of 1990." *Government and Policy* 13:459–78.

Smith, Bruce. 1992. *The Advisors: Scientists in the Policy Process.* Washington, D.C.: The Brookings Institution.

Smith, James. 1991. *The Idea Brokers: Think Tanks and the Rise of the New Policy Elite.* New York: The Free Press.

Smith, Jeffrey. 1981. "Acid Rain Bills Reflect Regional Dispute." *Science* 214: 770–71.

Soroos, Marvin S. 1997. *The Endangered Atmosphere: Preserving a Global Commons.* Columbia: University of South Carolina Press.

Spears, Tom. 1990. "Clean-Air Bill." *The Ottawa Citizen,* December 16, p. C6.

Stanfield, Rochelle. 1984. "Regional Tensions Complicate Search for an Acid Rain Remedy." *National Journal* 16:860–63.

_____. 1986. "The Acid Rainmakers." *National Journal* 18:1500–1503.

_____. 1988. "It's Hip to be Clean." *National Journal* 20:1510.

Steel, Brent S., Mary Ann Steger, Nicholas Lovrich, and John C. Pierce. 1990. "Consensus and Dissension Among Contemporary Environmental Activists: Preservationists and Conservationists in the U.S. and Canadian Context." *Government and Planning* 8:379–93.

Steger, Mary Ann, John C. Pierce, Brent S. Steel, and Nicholas Lovrich. 1988. "Information Source Reliance and Knowledge Acquisition: Canada/U.S. Comparisons Regarding Acid Rain." *Western Political Quarterly* 41:747–64.

Steger, Mary Ann, Nicholas Lovrich, John C. Pierce, John Klemanski, and Brent S. Steel. 1987. "Knowledge Holding and Citizen Influence in Environmental Policymaking: Canada, the United States and the Issue of Acid Rain." Presented at the annual meeting of the Midwest Political Science Association, Chicago.

Stern, Amy. 1986. "Clean Air Reauthorization With New Acid Rain Controls Approved by Senate Panel." *Congressional Quarterly Weekly Report* 44:2829.

Stern, Paul C., Oran R. Young, and Daniel Druckman. 1992. *Global Environmental Change: Understanding the Human Dimensions.* Washington, D.C.: National Academy Press.

Stevens, William. 1990. "Worst Fears on Acid Rain Unrealized." *New York Times,* February 20, p. C1.

Stevenson, Richard. 1989. "Concern Over Bush Clean Air Plan." *New York Times,* June 14, p. D1.

Sullivan, Robert. 1987. "Playing Games With Acid Rain." *Sports Illustrated,* May.

Taylor, Robert. 1986. "Appeal of Ruling Over Acid Rain is Won by the EPA." *Wall Street Journal,* September 19, sec.1, p. 11.

Thompson, John Herd, and Stephen Randall. 1994. *Canada and the United States: Ambivalent Allies.* Montreal: McGill-Queen's University Press.

U.S. Congress. House of Representatives. Committee on Energy and Commerce, Subcommittee on Health and the Environment. 1981a. *Acid Precipitation (Part 1).* 97th Cong., 1st sess., 1 October.

_____. 1981b. *Acid Precipitation (Part 2).* 97th Cong., 1st sess., 20 October.

_____. 1982. *Clean Air Act (Part 3).* 98th Cong., 2nd sess., 10 February.

_____. 1983. *Acid Rain Control (Part 1).* 98th Cong., 1st sess., 1 December.

_____. 1984a. *Acid Rain Control (Part 2).* 98th Cong., 2nd sess., 17 February.

_____. 1984b. *Clean Air Act Reauthorization (Part 2).* 98th Cong., 2nd sess., 22 March.

_____. 1986. *Acid Deposition Control Act of 1986 (Part 1).* 99th Cong., 2nd sess., 29 April.

U.S. Congress. House of Representatives. Committee on Energy and Commerce, Subcommittee on Oversight and Investigations. 1987. *U.S./Canadian Air Quality Effort.* 100th Cong., 1st sess., 2 October.

U.S. Congress. House of Representatives. Committee on Energy and Natural Resources, Subcommittee on Energy Regulation. 1980. *Powerplant Fuels Conservation Act of 1980.* 96th Cong., 2nd sess., 23 April.

U.S. Congress. House of Representatives. Committee on Foreign Affairs, Subcommittee on Human Rights and International Organizations. 1981. *United States–Canadian Relations and Acid Rain.* 97th Cong., 1st sess., 20 May.

U.S. Congress.   House of Representatives.   Committee on Interstate and Foreign Commerce, Subcommittee on Energy and Power. 1980. *Powerplant Fuel Conservation Act of 1980.* 96th Cong., 2nd sess., 2 April.

U.S. Congress.   House of Representatives.   Committee on Interstate and Foreign Commerce, Subcommittee on Oversight and Investigations. 1980. *Acid Rain.* 96th Cong., 2nd sess., 26 February.

U.S. Congress.   House of Representatives.   Committee on Science and Technology. 1984. *EPA's Office of Research and Development and Related Issues.* 98th Cong., 2nd sess., 14 March.

U.S. Congress.   House of Representatives.   Committee on Science and Technology, Subcommittee on Natural Resources, Agricultural Research and Environment. 1980. *Authorization for the Office of Research and Development, EPA.*   96th Cong., 2nd sess., 19 February.

————.   1981. *Acid Rain.* 97th Cong., 1st sess., 18 September.

————.   1983. *Acid Rain: Implications for Fossil R&D.* 98th Cong., 1st sess., 13 September.

————.   1985. *Acid Rain Research.* 99th Cong., 1st sess., 3 April.

U.S. Congress.   House of Representatives.   Committee on Science, Space and Technology, Subcommittee on Natural Resources, Agricultural Research and Environment. 1988. *National Acid Precipitation Assessment program.* 100th Cong., 2nd sess., 27 April.

U.S. Congress. Senate. Committee on Commerce, Science, and Transportation. 1988. *Impact of Acid Rain on Coastal Waters.* 100th Cong., 2nd sess., 8 June.

U.S. Congress. Senate. Committee on Energy and Natural Resources. 1980. *Effects of Acid Rain.* 96th Cong., 2nd sess., 28 May.

————.   1986. *Clean Coal Technology Development and Strategies for Acid Rain Control.* 99th Cong., 2nd sess., 9 June.

U.S. Congress. Senate. Committee on Energy and Natural Resources, Subcommittee on Energy Regulation. 1980. *Powerplant Fuels Conservation Act of 1980.* 96th Cong., 2nd sess., 23 April.

U.S. Congress. Senate. Committee on Environment and Public Works. 1980. *Economic Impact of Acid Rain.* 96th Cong., 2nd sess., 23 September.

————.   1981. *Clean Air Act Oversight (Field Hearings) Part 6.* 97th Cong., 1st sess., 14 April.

————.   1982. *Acid Rain: A Technical Inquiry.* 97th Cong., 2nd sess., 25 May.

————.   1983a. *Nomination of William D. Ruckelshaus.* 98th Cong., 1st sess., 3 May.

————.   1983b. *Acid Rain.* 98th Cong., 1st sess., 14 October.

————.   1984. *Acid Rain.* 98th Cong., 2nd sess., 2 February.

————.   1985. *Review of the Federal Government's Research Program on the Causes and Effects of Acid Rain.* 99th Cong., 1st sess., 11 December.

————.   1986. *The New Clean Air Act.* 99th Cong., 2nd sess., 25 September.

U.S. Congress. Senate. Committee on Environment and Public Works, Subcommittee on Environmental Protection.   1987.   *Health Effects of Acid Rain Precursors.* 100th Cong., 1st sess., 3 February.

U.S. Congress.   Senate.   Committee on Foreign Relations, Subcommittee on Arms Control, Oceans, International Operations and Environment. 1982. *Acid Rain.* 97th Cong., 2nd sess., 10 February.

U.S. Congressional Research Service. 1982. *Summary and Analysis of Technical Hearings on Costs of Acid Rain Bills.* Prepared by Larry Parker. Washington, D.C.: Government Printing Office.

U.S. Congressional Research Service. 1987a. *Acid Rain, DOE's Clean Coal Technology Program, and the Lewis-Davis Report: Squaring a Circle?* Prepared by Larry Parker. Washington, D.C.: Government Printing Office.

U.S. Congressional Research Service. 1987b. *Acid Rain Control and Clean Coal Technology.* Prepared by Larry Parker and Gregory Chin. Washington, D.C.: Government Printing Office.

U.S. Congressional Research Service. 1988. *Canada's Progress on Acid Rain Control: Shifting Gears or Stalled in Neutral?* Prepared by Mira Courpas and Larry Parker. Washington, D.C.: Government Printing Office.

U.S. Department of State. 1980. Memorandum of Intent Between the Government of Canada and the Government of the United States of America Concerning Transboundary Air Pollution. 5 August. TIAS no. 9856. *United States Treaties and Other International Agreements*, vol. 32, pt. 3.

_____. 1991. The Agreement Between the Government of the United States of America and the Government of Canada on Air Quality. 13 March. TIAS no. 11783. *Treaties and Other International Acts Series.*

U.S. Environmental Protection Agency. 1994. *United States–Canada Air Quality Agreement: 1994 Progress Report.* Washington, D.C.: Government Printing Office.

U.S. Environmental Protection Agency. 1998. *United States–Canada Air Quality Agreement: 1998 Progress Report.* Washington, D.C.: Government Printing Office.

U.S. General Accounting Office. 1981. *The Debate Over Acid Precipitation: Opposing Views, Status of Research.* Washington, D.C.: Government Printing Office.

_____. 1984. *An Analysis of Issues Concerning "Acid Rain."* Washington, D.C.: Government Printing Office.

_____. 1987. *Acid Rain: Delays and Management Changes in the Federal Research Program.* Washington, D.C.: Government Printing Office.

U.S. National Acid Precipitation Assessment Program. 1987. *Interim Assessment: The Causes and Effects of Acidic Deposition.* Washington, D.C.: National Acid Precipitation Assessment Program.

U.S. National Acid Precipitation Assessment Program. 1991. *Integrated Assessment Report.* Washington, D.C.: National Acid Precipitation Assessment Program.

U.S. Office of Technology Assessment. 1984. *Acid Rain and Transported Air Pollutants: Implications for Public Policy.* Washington, D.C.: Government Printing Office.

Vaillancourt, Jean-Guy. 1995. "Environment." In *Conservation and Environmentalism*, ed. Robert Paehlke. New York: Garland Publishing, Inc.

Vance, Cyrus. 1983. "Foreword." In *Canadian-American Relations: The Promise and the Challenge*, eds. Kenneth Curtis and John Carroll. Lexington, Massachusetts: D.C. Heath and Co.

Victor, Kirk. 1989. "Bad Days for Black Rock." *National Journal* 21:1988–91.

Vig, Norman, and Michael Kraft. 1984. *Environmental Policy in the 1980s: Reagan's New Agenda.* Washington, D.C.: Congressional Quarterly Press.

Wetstone, Gregory. 1980. "The Need for a New Regulatory Approach." *Environment* 22:9–43.

Wildavsky, Aaron. 1995. *But Is It True? A Citizen's Guide to Environmental Health and Safety Issues.* Cambridge: Harvard University Press.

Wilk, I.J. 1985. "Responsibilities of Scientists: Examination of the Acid Precipitation Problem." *The Science of the Total Environment* 44:293–99.

Wilkening, Kenneth. 1997. "Science/Politics as Ying/Yang: The Role of Scientists and Scientific Knowledge in Regime Formation on the Acid Deposition Issue in East Asia." Presented at the annual meeting of the International Studies Association, Toronto, Canada.

Williams, Bruce, and Albert Matheny. 1995. *Democracy, Dialogue and Environmental Disputes: The Contested Languages of Social Regulation.* New Haven: Yale University Press.

Winegard, William C. 1991. "The Canada–United States S&T Relationship in a Globalized Economy: Challenges for the 1990s." In *Canada and the United States in the 1990s: An Emerging Partnership*, ed. William Winegard. Washington, D.C.: Brassey's.

Winstanley, Derek, Robert Lackey, Walter Warnick, and John Malanchuk. 1998. "Acid Rain: Science and Policy Making." *Environmental Science and Policy* 1:51–57.

Yan, Norman, Wendel Keller, Norman Scully, David Lean, and Peter Dillon. 1996. "Increased UV-B Penetration in a Lake Owing to Drought-induced Acidification." *Nature* 381:141–43.

Yanarella, Ernest J., and Randal H. Ihara, eds. 1985. *The Acid Rain Debate: Scientific, Economic, and Political Dimensions.* Boulder: Westview Press.

Yearley, Steven. 1995. "The Environmental Challenge to Science Studies." In *Handbook of Science and Technology Studies*, eds. Sheila Jasanoff, Gerald E. Markle, James C. Peterson, and Trevor Pinch. Thousand Oaks, CA: Sage Publications.

Zillman, John W. 1997. "Atmospheric Science and Public Policy." *Science* 276: 1084–86.

Index

About the Author

LESLIE R. ALM is Associate Professor of Political Science at Boise State University. An expert on environmental policy making, his essays and articles have appeared in various books and journals, including *Canadian-American Public Policy*, *The Journal of Environmental Systems*, and *Science, Technology, and Human Values*.

ISBN 0-275-96916-9

HARDCOVER BAR CODE